RED RUM

A RACING LEGEND

RED RUM

A RACING LEGEND

Ginger McCain

Weidenfeld & Nicolson
LONDON

Contents

The Early Years

S urprisingly, yet appropriately as it turned out, the first time I ever set eyes on *Red Rum* was at Aintree.

It was the day before the notorious 1967 Grand National, in which a pile-up at the 23rd fence resulted in the 'no-hoper' *Foinavon* becoming just the fourth 100/1 winner in the history of the race.

The event that drew my attention to *Red Rum* that Friday in April was a humble Selling Plate for two year olds being run over five furlongs on the flat, and all the contestants were appearing for the very first time on a racecourse. Third in the betting at 5/1, *Red Rum* was being ridden by Paul Cook and, as is usual with two year olds at this early stage of their careers, he ran green until being driven along from halfway. Then, producing a determined run in the last 200 yards (180 metres), the leggy gelding got up in the final strides to force a dead-heat with the second favourite *Curlicue*.

All in all, it was a workmanlike performance and he was duly bought in by his connections for 300 guineas, but for such a young animal on his initial outing he had had a very hard race.

At the time, I was about to make the daring transition from mere permit holder to public trainer, with my interests very firmly founded in the National Hunt side of racing. Yet over the ensuing years, *Red Rum*'s name did crop up from time to time, particularly when he was switched from flat to jumping.

Bred by Martin McEnery in County Kilkenny, much has been made of the fact that *Red Rum* was intended to be nothing more than a sprinter. Although it is always easy to be wise after the event, a closer inspection of his blood-lines could indeed suggest that there existed some staying power within them – at least on the male side of his pedigree.

By the grey stallion *Quorum*, a former top-class miler beaten by only half a length in the Two Thousand Guineas by *Crepello*, his dam was *Mared*, whose career on the turf was ruined by her alleged madness. After winning just one small maiden stake at Galway, she was retired to stud, and *Red Rum* was her third foal. *Red Rum*'s grand-sire, *Vilmorin*, was a brilliant sprinter, but a further generation back to a great-grand sire produces that slender hint of stamina in the form of the 1938 Derby winner, *Bois Roussel*. At stud, this premier classic hero not only became champion sire in 1949, but also produced the winners of two Irish Derbies and, most significantly, the winners of two St Legers.

It was again at Liverpool races, in March 1968, that I saw *Red Rum* for the second time. A little more than an hour after *Red Alligator* romped to a 20-length victory in the Grand National, *Red Rum* was ridden by Lester Piggott in the one-mile (1.6-km) Earl of Sefton's Handicap Stakes. Carrying top weight of

A hard fought tussle

Red Rum battles on gamely under jockey Paul Cook to force a dead-heat with *Curlicue* in the Thursby Selling Plate. The date was 7 April 1967, this was his very first appearance on a racecourse and, most appropriately, the venue was Aintree.

8 stone 12 pounds (56.2kg), he put up a very spirited performance to get within a short head of the winner, *Alan's Pet*, to whom he was conceding 18 pounds (8kg). Strange to relate, the jockey who won the Grand National that day was a 20-year-old young man from the north east named Brian Fletcher.

After the excitement of the great steeplechase, it was back to work for me. Back to the used-car showroom in Upper Aughton Road, Birkdale and my yard behind it, which housed the 11 thoroughbreds then in my care. They were the property of six valued owners, one of whom was my wife, Beryl. In what must have been one of the least-distinguished racing stables in the country, we worked long and hard with a small but loyal team. The one thing we had in abundance was hope – yet that's a thing that won't put food in your mouth, or in the mouths of the horses. Money was extremely tight and although my part-time taxiing around the streets of Southport helped out, without the total support of Beryl I would have been lost. My constant assurances to her that when that 'one good horse' came into our yard we would be set, must have sounded like a never-ending pipe dream.

Second season success

Red Rum's first race as a three year old produces a victory in Doncaster's Waterdale Selling Handicap. Top weight, with 9 stone 2 pounds (58kg), he was partnered by Geoff Lewis.

In September 1968 it came to my notice that *Red Rum* had not only changed stables, he had also begun his jumping career. Still only a three year old, he had been bought out of Tim Molony's Melton Mowbray yard by the much respected veteran Yorkshire trainer Bobbie Renton, on behalf of his patron Mrs Lurline Brotherton. It was for this lady that Renton had sent out that outstanding Liverpool jumper *Freebooter* to win the 1950 Grand National. He was in the best of hands, for if the gutsy little fellow I had twice seen run so well on the flat had any ability 'over the sticks', then Renton was certainly the man to bring it out. Running in a field of 10 horses, for the £340 Junior Novices Hurdle over 2 miles 100 yards (3.4km) at Cheltenham that September afternoon, he was ridden by the reigning champion National Hunt jockey Josh Gifford. *Red Rum* once more put up a genuine performance in finishing second, five lengths behind the Fulke Walwyn trained *Acastus*.

Red Rum laughing

At a training session, *Red Rum* shows his teeth to the camera.

I suppose I was lucky that Aintree was my local racecourse, for had it not been that at Southport we were only 15 miles (24km) from the track, I probably would not have seen as much of *Red Rum* as I did. Sure enough, when the 1969 Grand National meeting came around, *Red Rum* paid Aintree his third visit in as many years, and this time for an event over obstacles. In his four races since that good Cheltenham effort, the gelding had recorded two thirds and a fourth, and on just one occasion had failed to reach the frame. Despite this, he was allowed to start at 100/8 in the 16-runner Lancashire Hurdle over 2 miles 100 yards (3.4km) on the opening day of the Grand National fixture. He ran a blinder under Paddy Broderick. Prominent throughout, he hurdled brilliantly, was still well there with a chance two from home and, although outpaced by the winner, *Clever Scot*, in the closing stages, was by no means disgraced in being beaten by ten lengths into second place. The jockey aboard *Clever Scot* was Brian Fletcher. Just 11 days later I was pleased to read that the promise displayed at Liverpool was amply rewarded when *Red Rum* won his first race over timber in the Bilton Hurdle at Wetherby. In quick succession two more hurdle victories followed – at Nottingham and Teeside Park – but in his final race of the season he put in a lacklustre performance, finishing down the course at Ayr.

As for my fortunes while *Red Rum* was establishing himself as a jumper, well, they could not have been worse. With one solitary winner in my first season as a 'real' trainer and none at all in the second, the prospect of finding that 'one good horse' seemed as remote as ever. Then an encounter with one of Southport's wealthiest residents, the elderly Mr Noel Le Mare, led to a brief spell of renewed hope. Most Saturday nights, the old gentleman was a passenger in my cab, and while driving him to the Prince of Wales Hotel all we talked about was horses. He really knew his racing all right, and so he should, for he had owned horses for many years and had even been represented in the Grand National a couple of times. It was Aintree's big race that most enthralled Mr Le Mare, and it transpired during our regular horsy talks that it had been his ambition to win the Grand National since he was a struggling youngster in Liverpool. One evening, this grand old gentleman bought two of my horses and allowed me to train for him. Although both were very cheap, it did seem that my luck had taken a turn for the better. To my horror however, both were disasters, and one even had to be put down after finishing second in a decent race. Things seemed to be going from bad to worse, and although we remained friends,

Over the ditch

A well-measured leap over the open ditch at Haydock Park, with Ron Barry in the saddle.

Showing the way

Ron Barry and *Red Rum* leading the field in a steeple-chase at Wetherby in 1975.

any suggestion that I should train for Mr Le Mare again was carefully avoided.

After his hat-trick of victories towards the end of the 1968-69 season, great things were expected of *Red Rum* in the next campaign, but for him, too, there was constant effort without reward. It was the year of the coughing virus and there is no question that the horse was afflicted, for he ran unplaced in 11 out of his 14 races. Bearing in mind that this was only his third season, 14 races in one term for an animal just rising five years of age is a heavy workload, particularly for a horse not right in himself. It was a most disappointing time for all concerned with *Red Rum* – all those races without a single win – and yet there did appear to be among those many wretched performances indications of a

A champion in action

Red Rum leading the field in fine style at Haydock Park in February 1975.

tremendous spirit. It came on his 12th outing of that dreadful season in a 3-mile (4.8-km) hurdle race at Perth, when, after an already punishing period on ground totally unsuited to him, and while still far from well, *Red Rum* ran a scorcher of a race to be beaten by just a short-head by *Tabix*, to whom he was conceding 4 pounds (1.8kg). This undoubtedly had been a very game effort. In half of those 14 fruitless races, *Red Rum* had been ridden by someone who had now become more or less his regular jockey, an Irishman named Tommy Stack, a rider making a name for himself on the northern circuit.

We persevered in much the same way at Upper Aughton Road, with plenty of hope and enthusiasm but very little cash. The used-car sales helped, as did the taxi cabs, and it was the latter activity that allowed my relationship with Mr Le Mare to continue. Naturally, it was the Grand National that was our main topic of conversation, and his enthusiasm for that race never for one second dimmed: nor, thankfully, did his determination to have a go at winning it. We were fortunate in having an ally in his camp, so to speak. His close friend, Mrs Doris Solomon, realized the hardship we were experiencing and at every opportunity attempted to persuade the old man to give us another chance at preparing a horse for him. I was constantly on the lookout for anything that might make a Grand National horse to tempt him with, while ever aware that the asking price would be the problem.

At last I came across what I considered might just be that horse – a nine-year-old bay gelding called *Glenkiln*, by *Arctic Slave*, coming up at Doncaster Sales out of the Hawick yard of Ken Oliver. The most important thing was that the horse was qualified for the Grand National and, almost as essential, that he might not be too expensive.

With the kind assistance of Mrs Solomon, I received permission from Noel Le Mare to be bid for him on his behalf. I duly set off for Doncaster full of hope, yet at the same time anxious, for there was a rumour circulating that *Glenkiln* was not fully fit. At the Sales I inspected the gelding, convinced myself that all was well and, in due course, he was knocked down to me for 1000 guineas. He was a good-looking bay with a prominent white blaze and one white fetlock on his off-hind and, on arriving back at Birkdale, he became the centre of attention. We had ourselves a real live Grand National contender.

By this time, *Red Rum* had graduated to steeplechasing, acquitting himself well in his first season over fences by winning three times and finishing third on seven occasions. But it still appeared he was clocking up an awful lot of mileage. During that term, Tommy Stack partnered him in 12 of his 13 races and, for a

NO NAUTHORISED PERSONS

brief spell before *Red Rum* became such an essential part of my life, the Irishman actually trained him.

Glenkiln settled in quickly to our routine at Birkdale, quickly adapting to his new surroundings as well as the strange location of his gallops. Without any alternative, my horses had always done their work on the beach. Despite the countless suggestions that it was inappropriate for thoroughbreds to be worked exclusively on sand, my head-lad, Jackie Grainger, and I never found anything detrimental to their wellbeing in this practice. Anyway, we had no option. There was no schooling over fences involved: there couldn't be, not on Southport sands; just regular, fast gallops along that wind-swept coast. Every morning we had to harrow long stretches of sand for the horses to work on. An added chore, but a very necessary one.

One of the least pleasing aspects, to me at any rate, of being involved in racing is the clerical side of things. Documentation of any kind has never been my strong point and for this reason alone I take my hat off to Messrs Weatherby, who, as secretaries to the Jockey Club, handle so ably the administrative affairs of all racing in this country. My aversion to paperwork, coupled with an

Upper Aughton Road Stables
The small stable yard behind the used-car showroom where, for five successive years, *Red Rum* was prepared for the greatest test in the world of racing.

urgency to insure *Glenkiln*'s inclusion in the Grand National line-up, led to a monumental blunder. It was an absolute nightmare. Unfamiliar with the entry forms for such a prestigious event as the Grand National – this was the first time I'd been privileged to have a runner – I filled in a form headed 'Declaration to Run'. The purpose of this form was, in fact, to declare a forfeit. In other words, I had withdrawn *Glenkiln* from the race.

Making friends

A quiet moment at the stables provides the chance to establish a new friendship.

It was absolutely mortifying to have lost through a silly error what was very possibly the one chance I would ever have to send out a Grand National competitor. Even worse, and considerably more important, was the shocking disappointment my stupid mistake would cause to that wonderful gentleman Noel Le Mare. I simply didn't know how I was going to face him, but Beryl insisted kindly and with her usual understanding: 'You go and see him now and get it over with.'

It was nearly midnight before I summoned sufficient courage to tell him of my blunder. In what truly seemed like the longest few minutes of my life, Mr Le Mare took the sad news like a champion. He appeared more upset for me than for himself, attempting in every way to put me at ease and console me. In those agonizing minutes that lovely man demonstrated what a really super person he was.

In retrospect, it seems so very strange the way things happen, and how the most disastrous of occurrences sometimes bring about a happy and successful development. This was certainly the case regarding my embarrassing *Glenkiln* incident, for if it had not been for that lapse of judgement, we would never have come across *Red Rum*.

While we were suffering tribulations at Southport, '*Rummy*' was well into his second term steeplechasing, and in this session he was regularly competing over distances of 3 miles (about 5km) and beyond. Running consistently well, he won twice at Catterick in addition to showing prominently in most of his other races. His toughest test to date, however, came just a week after *Well To Do* triumphed in the Grand National at Aintree, when *Red Rum* lined up with 16 opponents for the Scottish Grand National over 4 miles 120 yards (6.5km) at Ayr. In the eyes of many, it seemed an over-ambitious venture on the part of his connections, a view that was reflected by his starting price of 33/1.

Although still owned by Mrs Brotherton, the promising *Red Rum* was now handled by Anthony Gillam, at Oxclose, Ripon, but with the ageing Bobbie Renton in a sort of semi-retirement. With Martin Blackshaw in the saddle, *Red Rum* confounded all the critics in the Scottish Grand National by running a simply superb race, even though he was well down the handicap. Among the leading horses all the way, he took up the running at the 20th fence and was only overhauled at the penultimate fence. Staying on well, *Red Rum* finished fifth, less than eight lengths behind the winner, *Quick Reply*.

For a horse in only his second season over the major obstacles, and who was still only seven years old, this was a truly tremendous performance. If the running of the young, over-raced son of *Quorum* in the Ayr race was a shock to the pundits, there was an even bigger surprise awaiting them when the season ended. *Red Rum* was up for sale.

Summer break

Veterinary surgeon Ted Greenway plays host to the Grand National hero at his delightful home in Cheshire. '*Rummy*' spent many happy holidays here, always returning to Southport ready for another rigorous preparation.

CHAPTER TWO
Getting together

The seven-pound claimer

Under the watchful eye of Billy Ellison on *Red Rum*, Donald McCain junior 'guides' *Glenkiln* along a sandy stretch shortly before the 1973 Grand National.

Copies of the advance catalogue for Doncaster's August Sales showed that of three lots consigned by Mrs L Brotherton for disposal, Lot 43 featured the bay gelding *Red Rum*.

I could hardly believe my eyes, reading and re-reading the advertisement over and over. What I did notice, however, was the somewhat curious failure to mention that the animal was qualified for the Grand National. But doing some quick sums, adding up the prize money he had won, proved without a doubt that the horse was indeed eligible for Aintree.

Both Mr Le Mare and I were all too aware that *Glenkiln*'s qualification for the big race was running out, and even though he had done us proud with both a terrific run in the Topham Trophy Steeplechase over one circuit of the Grand National course and with a win at Cartmel, the prize money he had earned was insufficient to requalify him. There was a good deal of soul searching before drawing my owner's attention to *Red Rum*'s availability, but once again the 'guvnor' came up trumps. He authorized me to bid up to 7000 guineas to purchase the horse.

(*previous pages*)

Chasing the clouds away

Southport pleasure beach, and the big-dipper seems to be *Red Rum*'s target at the end of a training session.

Back to Doncaster we went, with hopes high and me just dying to get a close-up look at the fellow whose career I had followed so closely from his very first juvenile effort five years earlier. In the auction, the bidding rose steadily, with both Captain Tim Forster and Tony Gillam, the horse's most recent trainer, coming in at around 5000 guineas. Yet the more I looked at the gelding walking around the ring, the more taken with him I became. He looked really superb.

Having spent a good deal of time at second-hand car auctions, I had learned one or two little ploys, and at this juncture in the proceedings I decided to use one. As the bidding hit 5500 guineas, I shot straight in and, with one bid, pushed it up to 6000. Just as I had hoped, it sank the opposition, and at that price he was knocked down to me. I was simply over the moon, while at the same time scared to bloody death. Apart from on one other occasion, this was six times more than I had ever paid for a horse in my life.

On the journey back across the Pennines, all kinds of thoughts ran through my mind, not least the awesome responsibility I was taking on as the fifth trainer in *Red Rum*'s young life. I was also placing this duty on Beryl and the entire team at Upper Aughton Road. They were worrying thoughts.

Ever the gentle-man
Donald McCain junior presents the latest addition to the McCain family with a tidbit.

Red Rum's new home was a far cry from all he had previously been used to. From the serene beauty of the depths of the English countryside, he had come to a former brewer's stable block behind a used-car showroom in the middle of narrow streets full of back-to-back terraced houses, with the constant rattle of trains from the too-close railway line always there to disturb any dreamy moments.

When he came down the ramp of the horse-box and gazed around so regally at his new surroundings, amazingly I felt a strange shudder of pride run through me, a feeling that increased as Beryl, Jackie Grainger and young Billy Ellison surveyed the new boy with obvious admiration. It was clear they were thinking the same as myself. Here was a real racehorse.

Billy Ellison, as my best-lad, was put in charge of '*Rummy*' and was overjoyed at the confidence placed in him. Surprisingly, right from the moment he set foot in Birkdale, the horse seemed completely at home.

I don't know if it is true that pride comes before a fall; what I do know is that, if it comes, that fall can be damned terrifying. Two days after we brought him from Doncaster, *Red Rum* was tacked up with the rest of the string and taken down to the 'gallops'. Young Robin Greenway, the son of my vet, Ted Greenway, rode the horse for this his first exercise stint with us, and all went well until we began trotting on the beach. I could not believe it, or was afraid to; *Red Rum* was lame. God Almighty, I'd paid 6000 guineas for a lame horse. Oh my God! All the lads could see it as clearly as I could, he was definitely going short on that off-fore leg. In

21

Happy as a sand boy

Billy Ellison steers *Red Rum* down the dunes at the head of trainer McCain's string. This constant activity was beneficial in the strengthening of '*Rummy*'s muscles.

exasperation I told Robin to take him into the sea while the rest of them went through their paces. Unable not to, I kept glancing over at them, the horse calmly strolling through the waves with the surf lapping his belly. I was totally devastated. It's just amazing the shocks the human form can withstand. Having just experienced the worst one of my life, I was immediately subjected to another. *Red Rum* walked back from the eddying tide completely sound and, better yet, he trotted well, too. Thankfully, he's never suffered from lameness again, except for the day after his first Grand National, during which he had struck himself.

It was to be many months before I discovered what had apparently been common knowledge among some people for some considerable time – *Red Rum* had once pulled up lame after a race at Catterick and, on examination by a vet, was diagnosed as suffering from the dreaded pedalosteitis disease of the off-fore hoof. This ailment was considered by most people within racing to be virtually incurable. From enquiries I made from a number of people concerning his legs, the only information I received was that '*Rummy*' was a bit 'footy', or had flakey and shallow hooves. With the immense relief of seeing the horse return sound from the sea, I had a comforting recollection of witnessing, when I was a boy, many old broken-down horses between the shafts of shrimping carts working on this very beach. They were all cripples with dreadful legs, yet after a season or two of labouring in the sea, their limbs were perfect. What a quirk of fate that of all the places *Red Rum* could have gone to, he finished up with a trainer whose only gallops were the beach.

There were no further signs of lameness, nor anything else for that matter. *Red Rum* was working well and with a zest that was highly encouraging, and he justifiably became the star of the yard without even representing us on a racecourse yet. Everybody thought the world of him, and the little devil knew it.

At last the day arrived when *Red Rum* had his first race in the colours of Noel Le Mare. The venue was Carlisle; the race, The Windermere Handicap Steeplechase over 3 miles (4.8km); and the jockey, Tommy Stack. It was an anxious time for all concerned, and although as the trainer I was expected to put on a brave face and exude confidence, my butterflies were fluttering as powerfully as anyone's. That Saturday, 30 September, kicked off in the best possible way for us, with our *Gambling Girl* winning the opening event – a novice hurdle. An hour and a half later it was *Red Rum*'s turn, and he cantered down to the start looking an absolute picture. At 6/1 he was the outsider of the four runners, but he belied those odds during the race with a good display of clean jumping that kept him well in touch the whole way. From the last fence he stayed on to win by three-quarters of a length from the favourite *Gyleburn*.

What a day. The yard's first double victory, a smashing win for racing's most loyal owner Noel Le Mare, and *Red Rum* in the winner's enclosure with his new owner (and an immensely proud and gleeful trainer). Eleven days later it was a similar scene, only this time the racecourse was Wetherby and 'Rummy's

Flat out

Red Rum leading *Glenkiln* in a fast gallop along the beach.

winning margin was an emphatic 12 lengths. We waited a little longer for the hat-trick, a fortnight to be precise, at Newcastle on 25 October, and although this was a hard-fought victory, with *Red Rum* staying on strongly at the end, he was none the worse for his exertions.

Three days later the limelight switched briefly from the stable star to Mr Le Mare's other horse, *Glenkiln*, who made the short journey to Aintree for a welcome revival of the old autumn fixture. It was a most ambitious gesture on our part contesting The William Hill Grand National Trial Steeplechase over one circuit of the Grand National course. Not just because of the severity of the fences, rather more because of the quality of our opposition. The Irish class horse *L'Escargot*, a former dual Cheltenham Gold Cup winner, was top weight and favourite, while his fellow countryman *Black Secret* had already twice proved that Aintree held no terrors for him. He had finished both third and second in the last two Grand Nationals, and this form earned him second position

23

in the betting. *Specify*, the 1971 Grand National winner, was also in the line-up, together with some very good jumpers, such as *Fair Vulgan*, *Sunny Lad* and *Gyleburn*. *Glenkiln* found little support in the market, being easy to back at 16/1, but from 'The Off' he simply slaughtered the field. Making every yard of the running, *Glenkiln* made it all look so very easy, and despite blundering the fence after Valentine's Brook, he ran out a very easy 12-length winner from *L'Escargot*. The prize money of £4802 was the most I had ever achieved for any owner, and by another strange twist of fate this victory qualified *Glenkiln* for the Grand National. It was simply unbelievable. We now had two horses at the old brewer's yard in Birkdale holding the big Liverpool qualification, and both were owned by the man who, for well over half a century, had dreamed of winning the Grand National, Noel Le Mare.

Within the week it was *Red Rum* back in centre stage, this time for the 3-mile (4.8-km) Southport Handicap Steeplechase at Haydock Park. Again he won as he liked and returned home so well I could hardly believe it. While the ground was still good, I took him for his fifth race of the season, north of the border to Ayr, for the 3-mile 3 furlong (5.4-km) Mauchline Handicap Steeplechase. Tommy Stack was unavailable so I approached Brian Fletcher and offered him the mount. This was the beginning of a partnership that was to last for 'Rummy's next 27 races. Even with a new jockey on board, *Red Rum* followed

On the beach

Ginger McCain keeps a watchful, if humorous, eye on his most important charge from behind the wheel of his car. For many years, the trainer's string of horses was as much a part of Southport's sands as the seagulls.

his by now usual pattern, jumping well in a prominent position throughout, taking up the running three from home, and coming home six lengths clear of his nearest rival *Hurricane Rock*. An interesting aspect of this result was the inclusion in the field of *Quick Reply*, who had won the Scottish Grand National with *Red Rum* a close-up fifth. This time, the tables were turned in a very positive manner, with *Quick Reply* trailing home in sixth place, no less than 25 lengths in arrears of the winner. Five splendid victories in a row and *Red Rum* still looked cherry ripe, and by now he had, of course, risen in the handicap. With the onset of soft going, he was given a mid-season break, yet he still worked well on the beach each day. In fact, he was such a trojan for work and, because '*Rummy*' took such a strong hold, poor Billy Ellison's arms were almost pulled from their sockets. All the locals made a real fuss of him. Most had won quite a few bob on him over the last several weeks, and knowing he was being entered for the Grand National, an everyday question seemed to be what the latest ante-post odds were for him. Watching them each morning striding out at full speed, *Red Rum* and *Glenkiln* upsides each other, the wind-driven spray whipping up their manes and forelocks, really was the most exhilarating feeling I have known working with horses. To think that these two lovely, genuine animals were Grand National contenders sometimes raised goose bumps on my skin.

"I THINK GINGER McCAIN IS GOING A BIT FAR WITH RED RUM'S SECRET GALLOPS!"

The laugh's on them

Just an example of one of the many cartoons that the Grand National hero inspired.

With the turn of the year, we got down to some serious training. The Grand National was about three months away and the younger of the two contenders, *Red Rum*, was our main concern because, by now, we knew that he hated soft ground. Still, there seemed no way we could avoid it, at least for a couple of races, for above all else we couldn't afford any interruptions in his preparation.

At the end of January *Red Rum* took on three other horses in the Cumberland Grand National Trial Steeplechase at Carlisle. It was intended to be a re-introduction to his real work, and '*Rummy*' was a revelation. He turned in a truly workmanlike performance, which took him into third place, less than two lengths behind the winner *Bountiful Charles*. At Haydock Park a week later, on ground totally unsuitable for him, '*Rummy*' ran another blinder in another National Trial to get within five lengths of the winner, *Highland Seal*, who received 12 pounds (5.5kg) from him in the handicap. On the first Saturday in March, *Red Rum* contested his final race before Aintree, and this was a very tense occasion indeed, for the slightest knock or injury can completely upset many months of hard work and destroy any chance we may have had of getting him to Liverpool in the best condition. Again, the ground was against him, but another game showing brought him home in fourth place in the Greenall Whitley Steeplechase at Haydock, just eight lengths behind the winner, a very useful animal called *Tregarron*.

That was it. He'd come through his preparatory races with flying colours, he was sound, and there was still something there to work on. And with that tilt at

Talking tactics

A deadly serious discussion between Don and Beryl McCain, and Tommy Stack in the minutes before the race. It is at such moments that the tension is at its greatest.

the most severe test then looming just four weeks away, each day became more important than the last.

On the sands each day *Red Rum* was flying, improving all the time, and just relishing every moment. He'd been allocated 10 stone 5 pounds (65.7kg) in the Grand National, with *Glenkiln* just 2 pounds (0.9kg) more, and as each day brought us nearer to that spectacular event, everyone in the yard, and many more beyond it, were hoping and praying for decent ground at Liverpool.

Our wishes were granted, and the going for the race on 31 March 1973 was officially described as firm. The horses were safely boxed and sent off on their short journey to the racecourse in plenty of time, with Beryl and I being driven there on the 'big day' by our friends the Wareings. My first visit to that historic course had been during the early months of the Second World War to see Lord Stalbridge's *Bogskar* win the Grand National, and since that time the place had held a special meaning to me. Beryl and I were engaged to be married on Grand

Jackie and Red

Head-lad, Jackie Grainger's rugged features beam with unmistakable pride as he sits astride the stable star.

National day 1959 and saw *Oxo* romp to victory. Two years later, on our wedding day, we watched the lovely grey *Nicolaus Silver* earn his place on the winners' roll of honour. Now this – a day I had long hoped for without any realistic belief that it could ever happen. We were on our way to saddle, not one, but two runners in the greatest event in the racing calendar.

In the week leading up to the big event the betting odds had tumbled dramatically on *Red Rum*, and by the time we arrived at the course he was being quoted at around 12/1. Yet another reason for anyone connected with him to suffer from palpitations. Yet we had done all we could with the horse to prepare him for this, the supreme test, and I had been more than satisfied with his final work-out on the beach.

There was a total of 36 other horses running in the race that day besides *Red Rum* and *Glenkiln*, with the Australian champion *Crisp*, the former dual Gold Cup winner *L'Escargot*, the consistent *Spanish Steps* and another who knew his

What have we here?

Beryl and Don McCain show their hero the china figurine cast in his likeness. *Red Rum*'s comments were unreported.

way around the track, *Black Secret*, all in there with an excellent chance of taking the honours if the luck was with them. In the paddock before the race, Mr Le Mare, gentlemanly as ever, shared his time between both his jockeys. Brian Fletcher, who was familiar with the big occasion, having already won and been placed third in the race, was astride *Red Rum*; and the little Irishman Jonjo O'Neill, who was taking the leg-up on *Glenkiln*, was experiencing the thrill of the Grand National for the first time in his life.

A vital part of the team
Jockey Brian Fletcher, who rode *Red Rum* to his first two Grand National victories. He also won the race on *Red Alligator* in 1968.

CHAPTER THREE

The glory years

Thundering into Becher's

Charging towards Becher's Brook for the first time in the 1973 Grand National. The leader is *Crisp*, on the right, with *Grey Sombrero*, on the extreme left. *Red Rum* is perfectly placed, fifth from the left and just behind *Black Secret* in the spotted colours.

Watching the parade from the trainer's stand, with a lump in my throat and those damned butterflies fluttering away, was a strange sensation. Here I was, after all the years of obscurity and hardship, rubbing shoulders with the élite of British horse-racing. Yet, of greater personal fulfilment was the sight of my two runners making their way to the start of steeplechasing's showpiece. Each second seemed like an hour, as the horses turned, cantered back down to have a look at the first fence and returned to the start to be brought under orders.

After a delay of three minutes the starter sent them on their way, with a reasonably level break and to the customary yell from the crowds. They streamed down towards the Melling Road and the first fence. *Rouge Autumn* and *Black Secret* were the leaders over the first, where *Richeleau* was the only faller. The only other horse to come down at these early fences was *Ashville* two jumps later. With *Grey Sombrero* holding a slight advantage over the joint top-weight *Crisp*, 36 runners pounded towards the notorious Becher's Brook. Putting in a superb leap, *Crisp* jumped into the lead over the Brook, which claimed *Culla Hill* and *Beggar's Way*, and towards the outside *Glenkiln* landed a little steeply but safely just ahead of *Red Rum*. From this point, the giant *Crisp* proceeded to

make a procession of the race, being three lengths ahead of *Grey Sombrero* at the Canal Turn and with *Black Secret*, *Endless Folly* and *Sunny Lad* the next three in line. The remainder of the field was already well strung out at this point. *Glenkiln* was in 12th position, still just ahead of *Red Rum*, and so far they had both jumped well and were racing alongside each other, just as they did at their training sessions on the beach each day.

Returning to the racecourse proper at the Anchor Bridge, *Crisp* had increased his lead to 10 lengths, bowling along well within himself and jumping those big fences superbly, but back in the main bunch behind I could see *Red Rum* moving into a more prominent position. *Grey Sombrero* came down heavily at the massive Chair when in second place, and his exit from the race left *Crisp* fully 15 lengths ahead of the rest.

Over the Water Jump and the Australian front-runner was going even further away from them, followed by *Endless Folly*, *Sunny Lad*, *Rouge Autumn* and *Red Rum*. Unfortunately, *Glenkiln* was one of the casualties at the Chair, along with *Canharis*, *Proud Percy* and *Charley Winking*. Back out into the country and the fast pace set by the leader had certainly taken its toll on the majority

Chasing the leaders

Red Rum (number 8) lands safely over Becher's Brook first time around in the 1973 Grand National, with his stable-mate *Glenkiln* (number 7) a neck in front of him.

(*previous pages*)

Making the pace

English soccer ace, Emlyn Hughes, tries to match strides with '*Rummy*' at Southport.

33

remaining in the race, for they were spread way back like washing on a line. Over the 19th, a big open ditch, *Crisp* was so far ahead – fully 25 lengths – it began to look like he had slipped his field. But the nearest to him was *Red Rum* and I think that Brian Fletcher had spotted the danger of being so far behind a

Riding a finish

Red Rum lands running after the last fence in 1973, but at this stage he was still at least 10 lengths behind the leading horse, *Crisp*.

horse at this crucial stage of the race, especially one that showed no signs of coming back to them. Once safely over Becher's for the final time, Brian began an earnest pursuit of the runaway, who had widened the gap to all of 100 yards (90 metres). All the way back down the Canal side I could see that *Red Rum* was making a little bit of ground at every fence, but *Crisp* was not slackening and was an awfully long way in front. With two to go, the lead was now 15 lengths, with *Crisp* still going well. But Brian was at work now, and although the gap remained the same as they left the last fence behind them, *Red Rum* had begun a tremendous run. At the elbow, *Crisp* veered off a true line – the first sign that he may be tiring – yet his advantage was still a commanding one and my eyes were fastened on '*Rummy*'. The run he produced to the line was relentless and brilliant, only possible from a truly courageous horse. It won us the Grand National by three-quarters of a length from a gallant but tired *Crisp*. *Golden Miller*'s 39-year record for the race had been shattered by over 18 seconds.

34

It was sheer bedlam in the winner's enclosure and I was overcome by a surg-
ing sea of emotion. Laughter, tears, numbed disbelief and hands grasped in relief
as well as congratulation. Incredibly, the most relaxed character among all that
joy, laughter and excitement was the reason for it all, *Red Rum*.

We were the toast of Southport that night. Parties continued long into the
early hours and we were fêted wherever we went. And, of course, everybody
wanted to see *Red Rum*. After only a little thought, we decided the easiest thing
to do was to take him with us, and that's just what we did. Like the perfect
gentleman, *Red Rum* walked calmly up the steps of the Bold Hotel on Lord

A dream becomes a reality
Smiles all around as *Red Rum*
is led-in after his first Grand
National victory in 1973.

Street, down the red carpet laid out for him and into the crowded ballroom. The crowd went wild, cheering and applauding him, and all of them during the evening straining across just to touch him. The celebrations continued the following day, when Billy Ellison, Jackie Grainger and myself took 'Rummy' on a mini pub crawl. As the booze flowed copiously, the sight of so many faces made

The dual winner

Having just won his second successive Grand National, *Red Rum* is cared for by Billy Ellison and Jackie Grainger. With him in the winner's enclosure are owner, Mr Noel Le Mare, Mrs Beryl McCain (far left), Mr Le Mare's daughter (second from left) and Mrs Solomon.

happy by our success was an extra bonus to my weekend of total and utter delight. I think the only fellow not celebrating with us that week was the local bookie, for with *Red Rum* winning as joint 9/1 favourite with *Crisp*, he had taken a right old pasting.

With our season at an end, we sent 'Rummy' to our vet's home in Cheshire for a summer break, and with some time on my hands I reflected on what we had achieved with our most expensive racehorse in barely seven months. He ran nine times during that period, winning six races and finishing in the money in the other three. In financial terms, he brought in £29,646 in win and place prize money. In other words, he had repaid his purchase price of 6000 guineas with quite a bit left over for good measure.

By the end of the 1972-73 National Hunt season, the records showed that Mr Noel Le Mare was the leading owner, with a total of £34,197 coming from victories with three horses. In the top trainers' list, I featured in sixth position.

Party time

Completely at home among the revellers in the Bold Hotel

In cash terms, this translated into £37,040, coming from 18 wins with eight horses. By anybody's reckoning, this was quite a step up from the form of previous years.

on Lord Street, Southport just hours after winning his third Grand National.

(*above*)

To the victor . . .

A much deserved present of a
new car for Beryl from 'Ginger'
and '*Rummy*'.

The only slightly sour note at that time
was the suggestion among some gentlemen
of the press that our success in the Grand
National had been a lucky one, due largely
to a suggested 'unfair' weight concession
we received from the runner-up. I could
understand their sympathetic attitude to
the brave *Crisp*, who ran a splendid race,
but we won the Grand National totally on
merit, for the whole object of racing is to
finish first past the post. *Red Rum* did precisely that and, to my mind, in magnificent
fashion. Anyway, perhaps in the forthcom-
ing season we could find a way to make them change their minds.

We opened our campaign north of the border at Perth on 26 September, while
the ground was good, in the Perthshire Challenge Cup Steeplechase over 3 miles
(4.8km). Third in the betting at 4/1, *Red Rum* was top-weight with 12 stone
4 pounds (78kg). Looking really well, he was up with the pace all the way.
Striking the front after landing over the last, he won unextended by a length and

a half from the odds-on favourite *Proud Stone*, with the
third horse 25 lengths further back. Unbelievably, we
were subsequently disqualified for allegedly 'coming too
close to the runner-up at the last fence'. In truth, they
were close together jumping the obstacle, but there was
certainly no interference.

Three days later at Carlisle, again carrying 12 stone
4 pounds (78kg), there could be no question of getting in
anybody's way. *Red Rum* simply stormed in, 15 lengths
clear of his nearest rival.

There was a fortnight break until ''*Rummy's*' next
outing, which was at Ayr in the Joan Mackay Handicap
Steeplechase. And yes, with 12 stone 4 pounds (78kg) he
was giving weight to each of his seven opponents.
Prominent throughout the race, *Red Rum* took up the
running three from home and, resisting a late challenge
from the considerably lighter-weighted *Straight Vulcan*,
had a length to spare at the post but with a good deal in

hand. In the words of the sporting press, 'this was a fantastic performance'. One reason for their high praise was the fact that, even though he made a bit of a hash of the last fence, he knocked more than seven seconds off the track record.

It was immensely gratifying to see the horse in such good heart, not just on the racecourse but at home. He simply thrived on work, relishing the fast gallops along the beach and acting the goat by playing about up and down the sandhills. He really was a terrific character and, believe me, he knew what he was and just how good he was.

His winning ways continued up at Newcastle at the end of October, when, despite hitting the last fence, he hacked up again this time by four lengths. That hiccup at the final obstacle took not a quiver out of him. He was so brave and strong and so obviously enjoyed his racing.

His next effort at Doncaster was one I somehow regret subjecting him to, not because of the outcome but because it was a rather pointless affair after an

Post time

On his way to the start of the 1973 Hennessy Gold Cup at Newbury, in which he was just beaten by a short head by *Red Candle* to whom he was conceding a stone (6.4kg).

(*left*) **A double Rum for Beryl**

Mrs Beryl McCain flanked by the champion *Red Rum* and the orchid named after him.

39

Poetry in motion

A prodigious leap at the second Becher's Brook takes *Red Rum* into the lead during the 1974 Grand National. Horse number 30 is *Charles Dickens*, which eventually finished third.

(*above*) **Beach boys**

A beaming Billy Ellison takes his treasured mount for a walk past the sandhills after a training spin.

already busy season. Basically it was a match at level weights of 11 stone 10 pounds (74.4kg) between just two horses, *Red Rum* and his old rival *Crisp*.

The Australian horse had recovered well from his exertions at Aintree some eight months earlier and he was from the fine stable of that excellent ambassador of National Hunt racing, Fred Winter. '*Rummy*' was simply outpaced by *Crisp* that day, going under by eight lengths and, of course, the result absolutely delighted those who had criticized our victory at Liverpool, since it gave some credence to their claims that it was only the weight that had beaten *Crisp* in the Grand National. Never mind, we had more important things to concern ourselves with.

Ever since its inception in 1957, the Hennessy Gold Cup has proved to be a highly competitive event, always attracting jumpers of the highest standard and, of course, it's a most valuable race in terms of prize money. This, then, was the target for *Red Rum* as his final race before his mid-season break. It turned out to be one of the finest and most exciting races racegoers were to witness throughout the entire season.

Of the 11 contestants there were only two, *Charlie Potheen* and *Spanish Steps*, carrying more weight than *Red Rum*, and the former was the clear favourite at 9/2. It was a fabulous race to watch, with the lead constantly changing, the pace hot, and with bold jumping through its entirety. *Red Rum* gave a tremendous account of himself all the way and his fencing was brilliant. Jumping his way to the front four from home, he stuck to his guns when the lighter-weighted *Red Candle* headed him at the penultimate fence. Rallying in courageous style on the run-in, *Red Rum* regained the lead, was headed

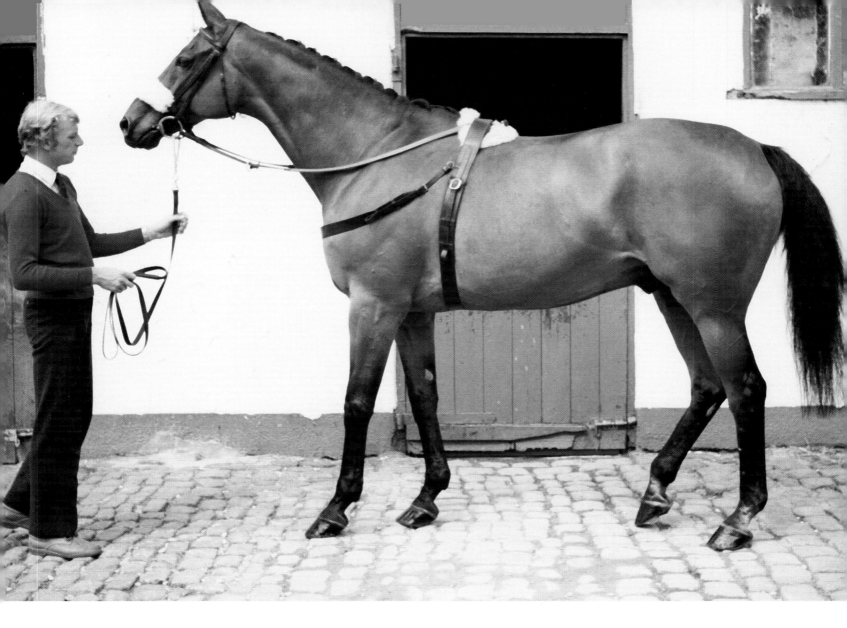

again, and still got his head in front once more. It was only in the last desperate strides of an outstanding contest that *Red Candle* snatched victory from *Red Rum* by the shortest of short heads. What a race that was and what exemplary bravery from two tremendously game horses. In no way had *Red Rum* been disgraced by the defeat.

As usual, he was his ebullient self the following day, bucking and prancing with Billy Ellison aboard, and one would never have dreamed he had been involved just 24 hours earlier in a tussle of such magnitude as that in the Hennessy Gold Cup.

Red Rum was, of course, entered for the 1974 Grand National in January, together with *Glenkiln*, and when the weights were published in February we were not surprised to see that 'Rummy' headed the handicap with the maximum burden of 12 stone (76.2kg). *Glenkiln* was far more leniently treated, being allotted 10 stone 2 pounds (64.4kg). We'd planned just two races for him before

Every inch a racehorse

A picture of health and fitness, *Red Rum* at home behind his trainer's used-car showroom in Upper Aughton Road, Birkdale.

(*left*) **Ruling the waves**

Cooling off in the powerful sea current at Southport after an early-morning work-out.

Here we go again

'Ginger' McCain leads *Red Rum* and Brian Fletcher towards the Grand National winner's enclosure for the second successive year in 1974. This was the first time the elusive double had been achieved since *Reynoldstone* in 1935 and 1936.

another tilt at the Grand National and the first of these was an extended 3-mile (4.8-km) affair at Catterick on 20 February. With 12 stone 7 pounds (79.4kg) on his back, *Red Rum* was giving fully 2½ stone (15.9kg) to four of his six rivals, yet after a two-month lay-off he performed like the genuine professional we all knew him to be. Moving up to the leaders on the final circuit, he bided his time until the final fence, then left them all toiling in his wake as he galloped away to an eight-length victory. Another super performance and just one more race between us and Liverpool.

Haydock Park is only a little further for us to travel to than Aintree, just down the East Lancashire Road towards Manchester, and on that first Saturday in March we arrived there to contest the Greenall Whitley Handicap Steeplechase. *Red Rum* was the picture of health, really on his toes and as fit as he'd ever been while in our care. Although we naturally hoped that he would give a good account of himself, our main concern had to be that he should return unscathed. All 12 runners jumped off well, making their way down to the first fence, which '*Rummy*' jumped in his usual steadfast manner. As they touched down and raced on, I detected some sort of scrimmage on the far side, and was gutted to discover that *Red Rum* was running without his rider. Another horse had cannoned into our '*Rummy*' from behind, giving poor Brian no chance at all of staying in the plate. It was a most disconsolate team that returned to Southport that day, but the important thing was that, thankfully, *Red Rum* had not harmed himself in any way while running loose.

Our arrangements for Liverpool were more or less the same as last year, including the training programme for our three runners in the Grand National, although this time *Glenkiln* was to be ridden by Reg Crank, with Richard Evans partnering our big race outsider *The Tunku*. It was interesting to note that *Red Rum*'s old companion Tommy Stack was on the favourite that year, *Scout*, a

Just another racing day
An informal moment for Beryl and 'Ginger' McCain at Aintree.

promising young horse from Arthur Stephenson's powerful County Durham yard. *L'Escargot* was taking his chance again, as were *Spanish Steps*, *Rouge Autumn* and *Sunny Lad*. The ownership of Aintree Racecourse had changed hands some four months earlier, when Mrs Mirabel Topham had sold it to Bill Davies, a Liverpool property developer, after almost 10 years of constant uncertainty concerning the future of the venue. It was, therefore, encouraging to note that Mr Davies was represented in the event, and that his colours were being carried by his recent purchase, *Wolverhampton*.

With all the preliminaries dispensed with, the 42 competitors took up their positions in the shadow of the vast grandstand, and in the final show of betting before they began their journey *Red Rum* was third in the market at odds of 11/1.

From the start, it was an almost trouble-free run down to the first Becher's Brook. The early leaders consisted of *Charles Dickens*, *Vulgan Town*, *Culla Hill*, *Rough Silk*, *Pearl of Montreal* and *Sunny Lad*, with only *Royal Relief*, *Go-Pontinental* and *Bahia Dorada* absent from the original contingent.

Over the Brook the 39 survivors leapt in near unison with, for once, not a single casualty at that dreaded landmark. Happily, our three runners were still in the hunt, with *Red Rum* enjoying himself about 12 lengths off the pace.

The scene changed dramatically two fences later, however, when no less than seven failed to negotiate the Canal Turn, among them *Rough House*, *Dublin's*

Green and *Culla Hill*. Two of the fallers here came down to the side of *Red Rum*, rolling precariously towards him, but with his perfect cat-like agility he had side-stepped them without any loss of momentum. *Pearl of Montreal* and *Charles Dickens* were maintaining a good pace up in front as they re-crossed the

Are the ears alright?

Lady Yarrow taking another close look at her model during her commission to sculpt the statue for Ayr racecourse.

Melling Road with a whole cluster of runners hot on their heels. As they lined up for the 13th fence, they were dangerously preceded by four loose horses. At this point, *Red Rum* was moving sweetly in about 12th position and *Glenkiln* was also handily placed just to his rear. Three of the riderless runners jibbed out at the 13th, but the remaining horse led the field over that and the next fence, and then on to the Chair

As *Charles Dickens* reached for the big ditch, the loose, pilotless horse swerved into him from his near-side and a pile-up appeared to be the certain outcome. It was only an outstanding piece of horsemanship on the part of jockey Andy Turnell that kept his mount, *Charles Dickens*, in the race. Stretching Over the Water jump, the running order was *Pearl of Montreal*, *L'Escargot*, *Charles Dickens*, *Sunny Lad*, *Vulgan Town* and *Spanish Steps*, with *Red Rum* in close touch and going oh so easily. Back in the country, the pace increased and, sadly, *Glenkiln* completely misjudged the ditch at the 19th, sending his jockey airborne to land on the turf. But ahead of him, *Red Rum* put in a prodigious leap, which placed him right alongside the leading runners. From here on, all the way to the finish, it was the essence of absolute delight to watch him. *Red Rum* took total control of the race.

Over the next two fences, *Vulgan Town*, *Charles Dickens* and *L'Escargot* each stepped up a gear in an attempt to match strides with him. However, when the magnificent *Red Rum* produced yet another brilliant leap at Becher's Brook,

46

their task became a forlorn one. *Scout*, the favourite, moved up threateningly as the remaining runners rounded the Canal Turn, yet even he couldn't get to '*Rummy*'. He pecked slightly on landing over the plain fence after Valentine's –

the one semblance of a mistake made in the entire race – but he never lost his rhythm. Back on the racecourse with just two fences left, there was only *L'Escargot* close enough to offer any kind of challenge. And try as the Irish horse did, there was simply no way that he could catch *Red Rum*. Running on strongly past the elbow, '*Rummy*' ran out a very comfortable winner by seven lengths from *L'Escargot*, with *Charles Dickens* and *Spanish Steps* filling the minor positions.

For the first time since 1936, and only the second time this century, the Grand National had been won in successive years by the same horse, and the huge crowds at Aintree that afternoon went berserk with joy.

Scotland's tribute

A very proud moment for owner Noel Le Mare and sculptress Lady Yarrow at the official unveiling of the *Red Rum* statue at Ayr racecourse.

Our whole party were overcome with exhilaration and pride for our so wonderful *Red Rum*, a true champion in every sense of the word. The endless radio and television interviews we endured happily yet somehow in a numbed state of euphoria. Amid all the congratulations, back-slapping and very kind words from total strangers all I wanted to do however was wander off down on to the course and be alone for a little time, to dwell in solitary wonder at the magnificence of this 'one good horse' to whom I owed everything. And where better to do so than on the area of turf he earned as his kingdom?

Incredibly, there was more adoration still to come, exactly three weeks later in Scotland at Ayr, in the Scottish Grand National, which unusually that year had a longer gap between it and the Liverpool race. From some quarters we were criticized for subjecting *Red Rum* to another hazardous task so soon after his Aintree victory, but the horse had come back from that race so well in himself that we decided to give it a try.

We'd been allocated 11 stone 7 pounds (73kg) in this race when the weights were published many weeks before, yet some official suddenly started quoting the rule book, and the upshot is we were burdened with a 6-pound (2.7-kg) penalty for doing so well in the Grand National.

So much for fair play. A weight of 11 stone 13 pounds (75.7kg) means we are conceding 15 pounds (6.8kg) to our nearest rival, and an incredible 29 pounds (13kg) to some at the bottom.

There was an unendurable delay at the start, which caused every jockey except Brian Fletcher to dismount; it was a wise decision on the part of our jockey, because without his partner astride him *Red Rum* may well have become fractious and upset himself. At last, they were off, with *Red Rum* hugging the inside berth on the rails, but fourth last. He was towards the rear of the 17-runner, 4-mile (6.4-km) race for most of the trip, then he began making a forward move at the 19th. Over the third from home he was lying second behind *Proud Tarquin*, ridden by that very good amateur Lord John Oaksey, and with *Kildagin* finishing strongly on the rails. There was an ominous gasp when *Red Rum* hit the second last fence and I could hardly bare to watch, but in a flash *Red Rum* was away in a burst of speed that I could not believe. Up and over the last fence, he actually sprinted all the way to the post, the winner by four lengths from *Proud Tarquin*, with *Kildagin* a very close third. For several moments I couldn't move. I seemed transfixed by a strange sensation of what I think is called *déjà vu* for the briefest of seconds during those last 100 yards (90 metres) as *Red Rum* hurtled so bold and free. It was that day again at Aintree all those years ago and he was a little two year old having his first taste of glory.

The ovation that day at Ayr was something to be remembered. The crowd went wild with genuine thankfulness that they had witnessed a most exceptional racehorse perform an exceptional feat. Everybody wanted to see him, to shake my hand and buy me drinks, and from the kind invites from strangers I could have spent a month in Scotland and still not satisfied *Red Rum*'s ecstatic fans. One of the many treasured compliments I received was from the rider of the runner-up, John Oaksey. He came to me after weighing-in and very sportingly said: '*Red Rum* is already assured of immortality.' Sir John Thompson, *Proud Tarquin*'s owner, was equally kind, commenting: 'It's a privilege to be beaten by a horse like that.' Such decent, generous and thoughtful people are what make National Hunt racing the sport it is.

Another fabulous season had come to an end, made so once more by that son of a 'mad' mother, *Red Rum*. And away he went for his holiday in Cheshire, leaving me to plan a fresh campaign and to ponder on what more we could possibly expect from this truly incredible animal.

On parade
Taking his place at the head of the parade of runners for the 1975 Grand National with Brian Fletcher in the saddle.

At the head of affairs

Brian Fletcher and *Red Rum* lead the parade before the start of the Grand National in 1976

Reverting to our usual pattern, '*Rummy*' came out at Perth for his opening race of the new season, putting up a good enough display to finish second in the race he had lost through disqualification twelve months previously. Then he romped home under 12 stone 7 pounds (79.4kg) to carry off the Joan Mackay Steeplechase for the second year running at Ayr, to the obvious delight of the increased numbers of people who had arrived especially to see him. The race-course executive at that venue had commissioned a statue as a memorial to *Red Rum* and it was well on the way to completion.

Rather foolishly I sent him down south to compete in the Charisma Records Steeplechase over 3½ miles (5.6km) at Kempton, and, as I'd feared, the right-handed track was thoroughly unsuited to him. He finished unplaced. Back to his true self on a course far more to his liking, '*Rummy*' ran a good third in the Sundew Steeplechase at Haydock Park in November, and that was it until after his mid-term break.

Such was *Red Rum*'s fame by now that we were inundated with requests for him to make personal appearances at garden fêtes, opening betting shops, supermarkets and such, and when possible we complied. It was at such functions that the character and wonderful nature of the horse was seen for the first time by so many thousands who had never been anywhere near a horse in their lives. He was always a perfect gentleman – attentive, gentle and proud to have so many people admiring him. It was a role that was to occupy a great deal of his time in the years ahead, and nobody could have been better suited to it.

On 5 February 1975 he ran a very good race in the Haydock Park National Trial Steeplechase, winning in fine style as if rewarding us for giving him a holiday. Back to Haydock for his final outing before the Grand National, he started favourite at 13/8 for the Greenall Whitley Steeplechase and was a little disappointing in finishing fourth – but at least this time he'd completed the course.

Again with 12 stone (76.2kg), *Red Rum* topped the handicap at Aintree. He started favourite at 7/2 and was giving 11 pounds (5kg) to *L'Escargot*, the second favourite at 13/2. The attendance that year was the smallest seen at the historic racecourse for a long time, due to the greatly increased admission charges imposed by the new owner Bill Davies. It looked as if the doubts

concerning Aintree's future were re-emerging. There was a delay of some fifteen minutes at the start when *Junior Partner* spread a plate, but it didn't appear to upset *Red Rum* or my other runner *Ballyath*.

At last they were on their way, with the Irish horse *Southern Quest* showing up prominently from *Glanford Brigg* in the early stages of the race. The field was reduced to 29 after two came down at the second fence, with a further six gone by the time they reached the Canal Turn. At the fence after Becher's Brook, *L'Escargot* made an horrendous and uncharacteristic blunder on the inside, and it was only the superb horsemanship of his jockey Tommy Carberry that kept the partnership intact.

Already I could see that *Red Rum* was far from running comfortably. In fact, he was hating every minute, simply loathing the soft ground. Approaching the Chair at the halfway point the order of running was, *Glanford Brigg*, *Beau Bob*, *Southern Quest*, *L'Escargot*, *Manicou Bay* and *The Dikler*. *Red Rum* was far to

Becher's Brook 1976

Red Rum lands safely over the testing Becher's Brook in the 1976 Grand National.

51

the rear with only five or six others behind him. Yet, surprisingly, by the time Becher's Brook was reached for the final time, he was well in contention with the leaders. Jumping the Brook a close-up third on the outside of *Glanford Brigg* and *Southern Quest*, *Red Rum* was back in the place he enjoyed being most, up front in the thick of things. Over Valentine's, with just five jumps left, *Red Rum* went to the front ahead of *Southern Quest*, *L'Escargot*, *The Dikler* and *Spanish Steps*, with *Glanford Brigg* dropping away to be replaced by the improving *Money Market*. Our brave fellow still held the advantage as they came to the penultimate fence, but I could clearly see that Tommy Carberry had not moved on *L'Escargot*, whereas Brian was already at work on '*Rummy*'. They were neck and neck at the last, with *Red Rum* touching down fractionally ahead of his rival but with that very long run-in still ahead of him. At that point, I knew we were in trouble. Receiving 11 pounds (5kg) from our horse, *L'Escargot* ran on to a 15-length victory, with *Spanish Steps* third and *Money Market* fourth, just ahead of *The Dikler*.

In spite of the natural disappointment, everybody took his first defeat in the Grand National well. He had again run his heart out and proved beyond any doubt that he ran a far superior race at Aintree than anywhere else. *L'Escargot* had won a well-deserved victory, for he had already finished second and third in the race and he really was a very high-class steeplechaser. *L'Escargot* was immediately retired from racing. I still believe, however, that with firm ground at Aintree that day, it would have been a different story.

Red Rum's last race of that season was in the Scottish Grand National, staged two weeks later. '*Rummy*' went off as the clear 3/1 favourite, and although he jumped well throughout the entire race, he was to finish unplaced some way behind the 33/1 winner, *Barona*.

During the 1975-76 season, we suffered the very unusual experience of running *Red Rum* 10 times without once leading him into the winner's enclosure. They were somewhat depressing times. In his first attempt that season, at Carlisle in late September, he ran a smashing little race to finish third just two and a half lengths behind the winner, and giving more than 2 stone (12.7kg) to each one of his rivals. Again at Ayr, a couple of weeks later, he was conceding lumps of weight to all when coming fourth, but he made a few silly mistakes that day and the effort was a little uninspiring. The Peacock Handicap Steeplechase at Haydock in October was his next venture, where he was again weighted more than 2 stone (12.7kg) above each of his five opponents, but this time he ran much more like his old self. Moving into a challenging position turning into the straight, *Red Rum* was simply cruising when he slipped up on the flat when lying a close third on the run to the third last fence. The race was won by an animal trained by Fred Rimell called *Royal Frolic*, which, five months later, was to triumph in the Cheltenham Gold Cup. I was aware that whispers were circulating that 'Rummy' was 'over the hill', passed his best, and that I was over-racing him, yet you will always find people who cannot exist without throwing out criticism in some direction. Rarely, however, is it at themselves.

All to play for

Red Rum in the thick of things just behind *Glanford Brig* and in front of *The Dikler*, in the 1975 Grand National.

Regrettably, the outcome of *Red Rum*'s next racecourse appearance brought about the severing of a partnership that had been highly successful, congenial and popular. The John Eustace Smith Trophy Steeplechase at Newcastle was the event that led to a most unhappy incident, with *Red Rum* the even-money favourite in a field of five. Lacking a little of his customary sparkle, he made several mistakes during the race and once, on the run for home, looked to have no chance of winning. I felt though that he would, if ridden out, certainly be in second place. Brian Fletcher made no move on the horse at the last fence and was beaten by a short-head into third place. Worse still, as far as I was concerned, the jockey expressed views to the racing press without me or the owner being present. This was in my opinion totally out of order. It was an unhappy incident that could have been avoided. It was also, alas, a parting of the ways.

Ron Barry took the mount on *Red Rum* in the Hennessy Gold Cup at Newbury, where our fellow performed moderately, finishing sixth to *April Seventh*, but on the long journey home to Southport that night I still faced the problem of finding a regular partner for *Red Rum*. Ron Barry was committed by a retainer to another stable and, therefore, would not always be available when we needed him.

Stride for stride

Red Rum on the left, touches down just ahead of Irish trained *L'Escargot,* but it is the latter who wins the race to the post. Ridden by Tommy Carberry, *L'Escargot* had previously won two Cheltenham Gold Cups and was a high-class steeplechaser.

It was an old friend from the past who next took 'Rummy' on to the track, in the form of the current champion jockey Tommy Stack. Although the race, The Sundew Steeplechase at Haydock Park, had attracted only four runners, many people turned up just to see two of the brightest stars the jumping game had ever produced. One was, of course, our hero *Red Rum*; the other was the

former dual Champion Hurdle winner *Bula*, making a new career for himself over the major obstacles, and odds-on favourite for this race. *Red Rum* went to the head of affairs at the fourth fence, jumping well and seemingly more than happy to be reunited with Tommy. From the third out, *Royal Relief* took over with *Bula* just coasting, and 'Rummy' starting to get outpaced. With all the fences jumped *Bula* exerted his superiority, racing away for an eight-length win from *Royal Relief*, with *Red Rum* two lengths further back in a far from disgraced third place.

While *Red Rum* enjoyed his seasonal rest over in Cheshire, a row was developing between the Jockey Club and Aintree's owner, Bill Davies. The row became increasingly bitter and infuriated the sporting public. It led to the announcement that Davies was selling the racecourse to the Irish property developer Patrick McCrea, and racing's governing body countered by threatening to transfer the Grand National to Doncaster. A solution was finally arrived at when the bookmakers Ladbrokes came forward with an offer to manage the racecourse for the next seven years. All who appreciated what a valuable part of our sporting heritage the Grand National is breathed a huge sigh of relief.

Back in training for the 1976 renewal of the great race, *Red Rum* seemed much the same as we had always known him to be. Full of himself, cocky and

Neck and neck

A classic shot of Tommy Stack and *Red Rum* taking the water jump on their way to finishing third in the Sundew Steeplechase at Haydock Park on 26 November 1975.

It's a bobby's job

Billy Beardwood leads *Red Rum* through the quiet suburban streets of Southport after a training spin. As usual, '*Rummy*' is under the watchful eye of his regular police escort.

mischievous, and thriving on the large amount of work we were putting into him. It was apparent, though, that the public were rapidly losing confidence in the old fellow, and very probably in me as well. This was reflected in the betting on the Haydock Park National Trial Steeplechase, in which '*Rummy*' was down the list at 7/1. Pushed along to keep in touch, he was with the leaders at the 11th fence and still moving quite well until making a hash of the 15th, after which he was never dangerous. Finishing sixth, he was a long way behind the winner, *Forest King*. This race brought *Red Rum* on well, and we returned to the racecourse on 6 March for the Greenall Whitley Breweries Steeplechase, for which he was top weight with 11 stone 13 pounds (75.8kg). Showing prominently from the start, he looked to be there with a chance entering the straight for the last time. But began to fade at the fourth last, eventually taking the fifth slot about 15 lengths behind the winner, *Royal Frolic*.

I was more than happy with his performance that day, for he had been in against some good horses, had jumped well and had left me with something still to work on in the remaining four weeks leading up to the Grand National.

Again we had two runners in the race, both at extreme ends of the handicap. *Red Rum* was carrying 11 stone 10 pounds (74.4kg) and *Meridian 11* carrying 10 stone (63.5kg). The latter was a nice chestnut nine year old we had bought out of Ken Oliver's yard to represent my owner Brian Aughton at Liverpool, and curiously he had beaten *Red Rum* at Carlisle early in the season.

It was another horse that had finished in front of us that was to be the 7/1 favourite for this year's Grand National, *Barona* – the Scottish Grand National winner. Of the old brigade trying again, there was *Money Market*, *Spanish Steps* and *The Dikler*, and among the newcomers there was a mare named *Eyecatcher*. She was to have the benefit of an extremely experienced jockey guiding her; our former rider Brian Fletcher.

Mercifully, there was no delay in dispatching the horses this year, and the 32 runners charged across the Melling Road towards the first, led by *Highway View*, *Spittin Image*, *Money Market* and *Golden Rapper*. *Huperade* and *Ormonde Tudor* came down at the first fence, followed two fences later by

Milling around

Waiting to come under the starter's orders for the 1977 Grand National. Little did the thousands of spectators realize that they were about to see history being made.

another casualty, *Merry Maker*, and then at the fourth by *High Ken*, who brought down *Thomond*. Becher's Brook put paid to the chances of *Glanford Brigg*, *Tregarron* and *Tudor View*, and at the first fence back on the racecourse, the 13th, our runner *Meridian 11* came to grief together with *Nereo*. From this point in the race, the leaders consisted of *Money Market*, *Spanish Steps*, *Golden Rapper*, *Spittin Image* and *The Dikler*, with *Eyecatcher*, *Rag Trade* and *Prolan* also well in attendance.

Not an easy chair

The halfway stage in the 1977 Grand National, with *Red Rum* (number 1) safely over the notorious Chair, the biggest and the widest of the obstacles on the course.

The order remained unchanged over the Chair, where *Red Rum* was swinging along nicely in about 12th position just ahead of *Highway View*, *Ceol-Na-Mara* and *Barona*. On the long run back out to the 17th, *Red Rum* strode out well, Tommy Stack noticeably steering him to the wide outside to avoid any trouble with falling horses ahead. *Spanish Steps*, *Money Market*, *Rag Trade* and *Golden Rapper* jumped in line-abreast over the ditch at the 19th, with our *Red Rum* tracking them in about seventh place.

Approaching Becher's Brook again, *Golden Rapper* on the inside held the advantage, but he clipped the top of the fence and came down in an ugly looking fall, leaving *Spittin Image* in the lead ahead of *Spanish Steps*, *Eyecatcher*, *Churchtown Boy*, *The Dikler*, *Sandwilan* and *Barona*. Still going the longest way around, *Red Rum* was a close fifth at the Canal Turn and close on the heels of the leaders. Approaching Valentine's Brook, he began to draw level with the leaders, *Spittin Image*, *Eyecatcher* and *Churchtown Boy*. At the last ditch, three from home, it was *Red Rum*, *Eyecatcher* and *The Dikler* all within a

length of each other, but with *Rag Trade*, *Ceol-Na-Mara* and *Barona* breathing down their necks, it was still very much anybody's race.

Racing to the final fence, it was Brian Fletcher with *Eyecatcher* on the inside, *Red Rum* and Tommy Stack placed in the centre, and John Burke on *Rag Trade* running on the outside, all virtually in a straight line. But jumping the last obstacle the better, *Red Rum* was the first of the three horses to land, and looked all over to be the winner. But how many times in the long history of this race has that punishingly long run-in changed glorious victory into gallant defeat? So it was to be again, history repeating itself in its cruellest, wilful way.

By the time they reached the elbow, *Rag Trade* had got our measure, drawing ahead for what appeared to be a comfortable victory. Then it happened, all in a split second and completely unexpectedly. *Red Rum* ran-on. He was coming again, stride by punishing stride, battling his way back into contention at the end of a lung-searing 4½-mile (7.2-km) exercise in bravery of the highest degree. At the winning post, *Rag Trade* prevailed, hanging on to his rapidly shrinking

Out on his own

Foot-perfect to the end, *Red Rum* clears the last fence in the 1977 Grand National to romp home to a record-breaking third victory in the race. Jockey Tommy Stack's smile acknowledges the fact that the horse just appearing on the left is riderless and, therefore, no threat.

Striding for home

Tommy Stack brings *Red Rum* up the run-in after the last fence, well clear of his field and about to rewrite the record books.

lead, to win by two lengths and provide his overjoyed trainer Fred Rimell with a record fourth Grand National victory to celebrate.

Three weeks later, *Red Rum* came out for his last race of a season devoid of victories for him, but in which he had won undying respect for his tenacity, courage and quiet acceptance of his rags-to-riches rise to fame. More through sentiment than anything else, the betting public made him the 5/1 favourite for Sandown Park's Whitbread Gold Cup, in which he would be meeting some old rivals, including *The Dikler*, *April Seventh*, *Rough House*, *High Ken*, and *Boom Docker*, and one he knew better than most, *Meridian 11*. In the race, he blundered away his chances at the open ditch, yet still ran well enough to finish a respectable fifth behind that good young horse *Otter Way*.

With his racing over with until the autumn, *Red Rum* was in greater demand than ever before as a guest celebrity at countless functions, and one of the nicest compliments he received among this clamour for his presence was an invitation to appear at Cheltenham in The Parade of Champions. Later, he was the star of the night at Wembley's Horse of the Year Show, at which the announcer's words of introduction were drowned by the cheers that welled up from the crowd when the spotlight fell on the horse they had all travelled to see.

As in the previous season, we kicked off the new campaign with a run at Carlisle, in which *Red Rum* scored something of a bloodless victory by 20 lengths from just two other runners. But at least it showed us that he was in good heart and fit, especially since he was carrying 12 stone 7 pounds (79.4kg) in that race. His appearance at the fixture had also swelled the attendance at the

60

pleasant little track. In mid October, The Charisma Records Steeplechase at Kempton Park was his target but, as on his previous visit there, he displayed his dislike of the place with a lacklustre performance. Despite this, he still finished in fifth place out of 12 starters, behind a good young horse of Fred Rimmell's called *Andy Pandy*. We were to encounter this horse again before the end of the term. Nearer home, at Haydock Park on Guy Fawkes day, '*Rummy*' gave what I considered to be a really cracking performance. Carrying 12 stone 7 pounds (79.4kg), and with Ron Barry replacing Tommy Stack, he took on six others in the Cheltenham Handicap Steeplechase. Looking splendid in the paddock, he was always up with the pace, jumped very well and gained third place behind *Even Swell* and *Kilvulgan*, beaten seven and a half lengths overall. It was a particularly satisfying run for me, because fully 35 lengths behind *Red Rum* that

The record breaker

Romping home to an emphatic 25-length victory from 41 other horses, *Red Rum* scores an unprecedented third triumph in the world's toughest steeplechase. It is no wonder that even the policeman on duty at the winning post is adding to the applause.

'Marvellous, bloody marvellous'

Stamping his greatness for a third time, *Red Rum* winning the 1977 Grand National.

day was his Grand National conqueror, *Rag Trade*. Another three-horse race followed, this time at Newcastle, and it was almost a case of 'after the Lord Mayor's Show'. *Red Rum* finished last of three. It was nearly as bad next time out at Haydock on 1 December, last of three again behind *Bula*, but at least we were beaten by a very good horse and we were much closer at the end. I don't really know who welcomed the mid-season break more, *Red Rum* or me. The snide critics were at it again, we were even starting to get malicious mail.

Back to business once more, on the final run down to Aintree, and we went to Haydock in early February to run in the Malcolm Fudge National Trial Steeplechase. Things had not improved, we came last of the six at the end of the 3½ miles (5.6km), beaten out of sight by the winner. Oh yes, guess who that winner was: none other than *Andy Pandy*. It was just inexplicable, the horse really was terribly well in himself, worked well and still displayed an incredible zest for life. His appeal to punters was at an all-time low, as we saw at Haydock on 5 March when he started at 16/1 for the Greenall Whitley Steeplechase. Jumping off well, *Red Rum* matched strides with the leaders until going to the front at the fifth, where he stayed until the ninth fence, and then began to lose ground. He was beaten before hitting the second last and finished sixth, some way behind the winner, *General Moselle*.

It was a refreshingly new-look Aintree that awaited us that spring. The entire three-day fixture was, for the first time, confined to jump racing and the prize money on offer had reached unprecedented levels. It was fast becoming a meeting fit to challenge the Festival fixture at Cheltenham, with the added advantage of having better drainage than that at the Gloucestershire track. Every event on each of the three days was a well-framed, competitive affair, and it was a most thoughtful gesture on the part of the racecourse executive to recognize 'Rummy' by naming the final race on the second day The *Red Rum* Novices Handicap Steeplechase. The quality of racing over the whole three days was excellent. A most interesting development occurred on the opening day, when *Churchtown Boy* won the Topham Trophy Handicap Steeplechase over 2 miles 6 furlongs (4.4km) of the Grand National course and it was announced by his connections that he would take his place in the big race line-up two days later. It was a most daring plan, but *Churchtown Boy* had won his race like a very good horse by 15 lengths and, what's more, he only had 10 stone (63.5kg) in the Grand National. Favourite for the race was the horse we had met a couple of times on

Thank you very much

After his record-breaking third Grand National victory, *Red Rum* returns to Upper Aughton Road to the most incredible of receptions. The excitement, joy and obvious pride in the faces in the crowd say it all.

Haydock Park 1978

Before the start of the Greenhall Whitley Steeplechase, *Red Rum* (number 2) and *Lucius* (number 4). Planned as his wind-up race before the Grand 'National, it turned out to be his last ever race, for he was withdrawn shortly before the big event through injury. In his absence, it was *Lucius* who won the 1978 Grand National.

our travels, *Andy Pandy* at 15/2, who was to my mind thrown in at the weights. *Eyecatcher* was back again, along with *Sandwilan*, *Boom Docker*, *High Ken* and *Spittin Image*, who had blazed a trail for a long way last year. Another innovation, and one that I certainly did not welcome, was the inclusion in the race of a woman rider, Charlotte Brew, who was to ride her own horse *Barony Fort*. As our party gathered in the paddock, we all admired the fine looks of our dear old 'Rummy', strolling round that oval path he knew so well. It suddenly dawned on me that this was the fifth year on the trot we had stood like this, dreading the seconds passing while, at the same time, wishing that it was all over, hoping for the best while fearing the worst. It seemed, when looked at like that, that we must be bloody masochists, but I wouldn't have had it any other way.

As usual there was an abundance of forced laughter all around, and the realization was strangely comforting, since it showed us that we were not the only ones the tension was getting to. At last came the time for parting, the jockeys mounted and became as one with the horses beneath them, and we joined the ruck in the fearsome dash for a good vantage point. Please God, when this greatest test is over, whatever the result, let them come back safe and sound. Such maudlin thoughts have no logic in the cut and thrust of sport, but at times like these, in our inner depths they linger.

As they milled around before coming into line, I spotted *Red Rum* over by the far rail, looking superb, and he knew he did. Strutting around regally, as if surveying the opposition and informing them that he'd been here before, he knew what it was all about, had done it and, yes, could do it again.

They're off! The roar was deafening, but peculiarly in harmony with the twang of the barrier, and the waiting was at last over. Seven of the 42 runners fell at the first fence, where *Sebastian* V showed the way ahead of *Brown Admiral*, *Sandwilan*, *Roman Bar* and *Hidden Value* and the whole field was stretched across the full width of the course. At the third, the first open ditch, the Cheltenham Gold Cup winner *Davy Lad* came down, as did *Royal Thrust*, *Inycarra* and *Burrator*, and the leader was still *Sebastian* V. Another two exited at the next, *Fort Vulgan* being brought down through the fall of *Harban*. And then they were racing to Becher's Brook with *Sebastian* V really piling on the pace. But he treated the jump too flippantly and crashed to the

ground. *Winter Rain* and *Castleruddery* also departed here while, in mid-division, *Red Rum* was jumping brilliantly. At the Canal Turn the order was *Boom Docker*, *Brown Admiral*, *Hidden Value*, *Prince Rock*, *Forest King* and *Sage Merlin*, and behind them the rest of the horses were strung out a long way back.

By the time they crossed the Melling Road at Anchor Bridge, *Prince Rock* had departed from the race and *Boom Docker* had opened up a very long lead. He was followed back on to the racecourse by *Sage Merlin*, *Hidden Value*, *Andy Pandy*, *Roman Bar*, *Brown Admiral*, *Sir Garnet*, *What A Buck* and the improving *Red Rum*. They held these positions coming into the Chair, where *Sage Merlin* came to grief. By this time, *Boom Docker* had gone even further ahead of the field. Back out into the country, *Boom Docker* was an incredible 40 lengths in front of his nearest rival, but he shortened his stride as he neared the wings of the 17th jump and very deliberately pulled himself up. *Andy Pandy* was now left in front and John Burke, his jockey, kicked-on to increase his advantage. With a succession of perfect leaps, *Andy Pandy* approached the second

The doubtful runner

Back at Aintree, just 24 hours before the 1978 Grand National, *Red Rum* is returning to his box after an exercise gallop. With a doubt about his fitness, he was withdrawn from the race later in the day.

Becher's fully 12 lengths ahead of *What A Buck, Nereo, Red Rum, Happy Ranger, Churchtown Boy, Sir Garnet, Brown Admiral* and *Hidden Value*. He rose well at the Brook but his hind legs clipped the top of the fence and *Andy Pandy* fell, joined within seconds on the ground by *Nereo* and *Brown Admiral*. Almost within the twinkling of an eye, the whole complexion of the race changed. *Red Rum* was now in front, probably earlier than Tommy Stack would have wanted, but, like the true professional that he is, he accepted the situation. They skipped over the 23rd, a loose horse alongside them, and straightened up for the Canal Turn. In an attempt to shake off the riderless animal dangerously close on his inside, before making that acute turn ahead of them, Tommy urged 'Rummy' on. The brave old fellow sprinted forward instantly, jumped over and around to the left, and raced on. Hot in pursuit came *Churchtown Boy, What A Buck, Happy Ranger, The Pilgarlic, Eyecatcher, Hidden Value* and *Forest King*.

Over Valentine's and on he galloped relentlessly, sheer poetry in motion. Just watching him leap those big fences down the side of the canal so boldly and true brought a lump to my throat. But there was still a long way to go. *Churchtown Boy* was moving up dangerously and still full of running. Remember, this was not an ordinary race. Above all else, it was the Grand National, where anything can, and too often does, happen. Across the Melling Road for the final time, two loose horses had by now joined issue with *Red Rum*, their task fruitless but seemingly content merely to be in his presence. And still ominously close was *Churchtown Boy*, the only danger to a record-breaking performance, and a very real one at that. Just two fences were left in this epic race and, as they measured up for the penultimate jump, *Churchtown Boy* was within two lengths of *Red Rum*, with his jockey Martin Blackshaw not yet having moved a muscle.

They rose to the fence, *Red Rum* as fluent as ever, but the challenger fiddled it and lost some of his impetus. Our fellow was away, striding out majestically towards the everlasting glory that awaited him beyond that one remaining barrier of spruce.

The gap between *Red Rum* and his pursuer had widened, in a few well-spread strides, to six lengths by the time he, straight as an arrow, produced that last immaculate leap. For the briefest of seconds the gallant *Churchtown Boy* tried to get back on terms, but despite receiving 22 pounds (10kg) from the horse in front, it was an unequal contest. At the elbow, with just over 200 yards (180 metres) left, *Red Rum* produced the concluding stamp of his greatness, miraculously sprinting yet again to secure an overwhelming 25-length victory.

(*right*) **Riderless**

The Grand National 1978 and *Red Rum* is a non-starter after a late injury leads to his withdrawal. However, he thrills the crowds by leading the parade of runners, the first of many occasions he was to do so.

Churchtown Boy was second, followed in by *Eyecatcher* and *The Pilgarlic*, with the remaining seven finishers sadly unnoticed in the midst of the roaring excitement our history-maker had produced.

As the vast crowd went wild with frenzied delight, poor Beryl struggled at the head of *Red Rum*, actually trotting to keep pace with him on the lead-in to the

winner's enclosure. Tears of uncontrollable emotion, numbed expressions of amazement and open-arm welcomes of congratulation surrounded us in that seething mass of joyful humanity.

Interview followed interview, for the world's press, radio and television, and when BBC *Grandstand*'s Frank Bough pointed his mike in my direction, my initial words were a spontaneous and heartfelt: 'Bloody marvellous!'

I listened with pride as Tommy Stack expressed his feelings with his delightfully gentle Irish brogue. 'He's a tremendous horse around here and anything I could say wouldn't do him justice. The only anxious moment that I had was at

Becher's second time. The horse in front of me, the leader, fell, and I just went to the other side of him; then there was a loose horse coming with me at the Canal Turn and I had to race him to get to the Canal in case he shot across me to the right. So I just raced him and jumped the Canal slightly in front. He's like a ballet dancer, when horses fall near him, he just side-steps 'em. It was landing over Becher's that I began to hear this extraordinary roar, everyone at every fence began to shout: "Come on *Red Rum*. Come on *Red. Red Rum, Red Rum*." It was quite fantastic. He is a different being.'

Even in his moment of despair, jockey Martin Blackshaw, who rode the runner-up, found words of praise for the horse who had denied him success.

'Three fences out I thought "We'll eat *Red Rum*", but *Churchtown Boy* made a mistake at the second last and that finished him. Even so, the turn of foot that winner produced had to be seen to be believed, he just left us for dead. He's a truly tremendous animal and just about unbeatable at Liverpool.'

The reception awaiting us at Upper Aughton Road was fantastic. The police actually had to close the road because there were so many people jam-packed in a screaming, laughing throng. They were all so very kind with their praise and their generous good wishes.

It was the same all over again two weeks later up at Ayr, where '*Rummy*' went out favourite for the Scottish Grand National, and although he was never really in the hunt, finishing 11th behind *Sebastian* V, the crowd really took him to their hearts.

Nobody on earth could have deserved the summer break he got that year at Ted Greenaway's more, and he came back in his usual high spirits, ready for the season ahead. Adopting the usual pattern, he went to Carlisle in September, finishing a decent second to *Cumbria*; a close-up second next time at Wetherby proved that he was still enjoying his racing, and then, at the end of October, he ran fourth at Catterick. Back in action in February at Haydock Park for their National Trial, he was a disappointment. The old fellow finished a tailed-off fourth behind *Tregarron*. Due to injury, Tommy Stack had been unable to ride *Red Rum* in these first races of the season, his replacement being Ron Berry. But Tommy was back in the saddle for the return to Haydock in the Greenall Whitley Breweries Steeplechase. In the circumstances, although we didn't know it at the time, it was an appropriate reunion.

Again '*Rummy*' ran sluggishly, at the long odds of 33/1, getting around to finish sixth some distance in arrears of the winner *Rambling Artist*. Second was a nice young horse belonging to Gordon Richards called *Lucius*.

(*right*) **Just a spectator**
Billy Beardwood, *Red Rum*'s lad, looks forlorn with his charge in Paddock Yard, at Aintree in 1978.

Red Rum worked well in the days leading up to the 1978 Grand National, galloping along the beach at the head of the string, skipping through the sand-hills and giving us hope for the sixth successive year that yet again he would show them all the way to jump those enormous fences. Sadly it was not to be.

Having done a good gallop at the racecourse the day before the race, he was being led away to his box when I detected the faintest trace of lameness. The only other person there who noticed anything untoward was Peter O'Sullevan. The vet's diagnosis was a stress fracture of a small bone in the foot, and he warned us that the bone could collapse during the hurly-burly of such a gruelling race. If that happened, there would be no alternative but to put him down. Mr Le Mare and I discussed the problem and decided that it wasn't worth the risk. *Red Rum* meant too much to all of us and, indeed, to the whole nation.

Red Rum was withdrawn at about 7:30 in the evening, the night before the Grand National was to be run, he had run his last race.

CHAPTER FOUR

Honourable retirement

(previous pages)

A winning team

In his new role as hack *Red Rum* carries his trainer.

Day tripper

Red Rum and Billy Beardwood tread a careful path among their rapturous fans on Southport promenade.

On the morning of April fools day 1978, the front pages of every newspaper in the land screamed out the information that *Red Rum* would not be taking part in the Grand National that afternoon. From the very moment we announced his withdrawal and retirement, the media bombarded us non-stop. Late into the night we answered their questions, assured them that *Red Rum* was not going to be put down and catalogued for them his illustrious racing record. Their appetite for even the slightest detail about the horse was voracious.

Even when we arrived at Aintree, there was little let up in the clamour for news concerning '*Rummy*'. It was a generous, if novel, suggestion by the racecourse executive that *Red Rum* should lead the parade of runners before the big race and, of course, we had to comply. The lads took so much trouble preparing him, you would have thought that he was going to meet the Queen. But he really did look superb in every way when the time came for him to 'meet his

public'. The late withdrawal of our horse had left Tommy Stack without a mount in the race until, at the very last minute, he was offered the ride on *Hidden Value*. Before they left the paddock, we wished Tommy well on the horse that had run so well last year.

It was strange to see *Red Rum* at the head of the 37 runners, striding down that straight he knew so well, with such self-assurance but, oddly, without a jockey on his back. Cocking his head this way and that greeting the cheering crowds in the stands and enclosures was, I suppose, his way of acknowledging their adoration, and the spectators loved every minute of it. So, too, did *Red Rum*, who simply lapped up all that attention, like the great showman he undoubtedly was.

He was taken to the side, just beyond the Chair fence, while the competitors turned and cantered back to the start and when the last of them, *Sadale* VI, was completely clear *Red Rum* began his solitary walk back towards the stables. Just as the crowd had shifted their gaze to the milling horses who were awaiting

Street wise

Dwarfed by his mounted-police escort, *Red Rum* once more becomes the centre of attention on the streets of Britain.

(*right*) **A man for all seasons**
The smiling face of Donald
'Ginger' McCain.

the starters instructions, '*Rummy*' suddenly grabbed back their attention in the most audacious manner. The place came alive with cheering, yells and clapping as he pranced and bucked his way down that strip of green that had

The spoils of victory

A most impressive display of
the trophies won by *Red Rum*
'over the sticks'. 'Ginger' McCain
is in the centre and Tommy
Stack is second from the left.

been the stage of his finest moments in racing. It was as if he had rehearsed this a thousand times. He was a complete show-off, playing to his audience. To me, watching that incredible horse with moist eyes, it was a triumphal passing of a truly great champion, determined to flaunt one final time the prowess he had displayed so often in front of those ancient stands.

And then he was gone, and the race began without him.

The big winner that day was *Lucius*, the horse from Cumbria who had finished in front of us in *Red Rum*'s last ever race at Haydock. He stayed on well

at the end for a narrow victory from *Sebastian* V and *Drumroan* – just the sort of climax to the event that '*Rummy*' would have relished.

So began the whirligig of *Red Rum*'s social life, and he really did take to it like the grand old trouper we'd always known him to be. Requests came from far and wide for his presence at functions as varied in their purpose as they were in their locations. It rapidly became a full-time job controlling his engagements and preparing the old chap for his journeys, and in between time '*Rummy*' still led out the first lot, echoing the order of his previous lifestyle.

It was only now that I was able to indulge myself in my long-held wish actually to ride *Red Rum* myself, for right from the start I had made a private pledge never to sit astride him until his racing days were over. As my hack on the gallops he, too, gratified himself, more often than not at my expense. He would

A 'talking' horse

Trainer 'Ginger' McCain shares the humour as former jockey Richard Pitman tries to interview *Red Rum* from the saddle. It was Richard Pitman who was deprived of victory in the 1973 Grand National when '*Rummy*' got up close to home to beat him and his mount, *Crisp*.

gambol about, bucking and tossing with his usual, humorous high spirits, as if determined to show the long-legged character on his back that I was taking uninvited liberties. At times he could be an absolutely bloody idiot, but it was just his way, I suppose, of having some fun, and he was certainly entitled to that.

Regal escort for a champion

On his many visits to London, *Red Rum* was the guest of honour in the stables of the Household Cavalry.

Sadly, yet necessarily, our 'fun' together was brought to an end approaching his 21st birthday, when he started becoming somewhat distressed and sweating up heavily. It was discovered that an artery had contracted in his off-hind and he was developing a blockage. I never rode him again. Despite his mickey-taking of those closest to him, to his 'public' the horse remained and behaved always the

(*previous page*)

Champion partnership

The many times champion National Hunt jockey, Peter Scudamore, teams up with *Red Rum* at a function in the Pine Woods Restaurant, Formby. Peter had his first ride in the Grand National four years after *Rummy's* final victory in 1977.

consummate gentleman. Opening supermarkets or betting-shops or attending garden parties, his decorum was admired and marvelled at by the many thousands who clamoured to see him. From every section of society they came to stroke and pet him, or merely to stand for a while close to the horse who had achieved so much and, in so doing, had become a legend.

Red Rum's fame had spread far, far beyond these shores. Many times we received telegrams from captains of ships plying their trade on distant oceans, congratulating us on the exploits of the horse; and we even heard of a captain of an airplane using the craft's tannoy system to blast the news of '*Rummy's*' historic third victory to his passengers while flying over the North Pole.

Then came the visit of the Japanese-American businessman Rocky Aoki with an offer to buy *Red Rum* for $1,000,000. His company, Benihana of Tokyo, apparently opened a new restaurant somewhere every week and they wanted the horse to promote their interests. The answer to his offer was of course, no thank you.

A civic reception was given for our champion at Southport town hall, and the streets on the route that day were so crowded that the traffic had to be diverted. At the reception, '*Rummy*' was honoured by being granted the Freedom of Southport beach. We still have the extremely impressive looking scroll which is signed by the Chairman of Tourism, Mr R E Gregson.

Journeying a short way up the coast to Blackpool one autumn, *Red Rum* was the guest of honour at the traditional ceremony of switching on the illuminations. It was conducted from the town tall. With Tommy Stack once more in the saddle, *Red Rum* sedately passed through a beam to light up the whole of that bustling seaside resort.

One of his most amazing appointments in those days of honourable retirement, even for us at the yard who knew him so well, was the night he made his grand entrance in front of a distinguished assembly at the BBC's Sports Review of the Year, held on the second floor of the New London Theatre. We had been rather concerned about his route to the stage, since it involved using a lift never designed for anything as big, or potentially fractious, as our equine passenger. *Red Rum* did, however, somehow realize the importance of the occasion – or perhaps, in that so uncannily astute brain of his, he guessed that the television cameras were waiting for him. To the most affectionate applause from so many seasoned professional athletes, he strode to centre stage and stood looking simply magnificent, as if it were the most normal thing in the world for him to be there. They had erected a huge screen, on which Tommy Stack, at that time in a wheelchair because of a racing accident, suddenly appeared. As Tommy began answering Frank Bough's questions, *Red Rum* cocked his ears in that knowing way of his and

'How tickled I am'
King of the Diddymen, Ken Dodd, meets the King of Aintree. Jonjo O'Neill is acting as the interpreter.

turned his face to the screen, listening to the praise his former partner heaped on him. That simple and so spontaneous act of recognition on the part of a

horse for his former friend and companion just brought the house down and was, of course, marvellous television.

Each spring he returned to the place he knew so well, and at which he was so loved and revered – Aintree racecourse. Leading the parade of Grand National runners had by now become something of an annual tradition, and on several occasions we had a stable-mate of his among the competitors behind him. One year, a suggestion was made by a member of the race organizers that his services in this role should be dispensed with. There followed such an outburst of protest from the public that the idea was dropped, never to be raised again. In 1988, Aintree Racecourse Company, together with the Grand National sponsors, Seagram UK Ltd, paid their own special tribute to the great horse. Unveiled that year, and sited midway between the paddock and the winner's enclosure, was the excellent bronze statue of *Red Rum* by Philip Blacker. The choice of sculptor for this work could not have been more appropriate, for quite apart from Phil's obvious artistic talent, he was formerly a steeplechase jockey. He rode *Spanish Steps* into fourth place behind *Red Rum* in the 1973 Grand National, and was subsequently also in the frame when finishing third and fourth in the race. It was a right Royal celebration that day in 1988, with HRH The Princess Royal performing the unveiling – the only sadness was that our old friend and benefactor Noel Le Mare was not there. He had died in 1979.

Seeing that statue gives me enormous pride each time I approach it. The like-ness to 'Rummy' is so accurate; that cocky stance, arched neck, with his head and ears cocked and those knowing eyes gazing, just the way they so often did, towards the sky.

Early in 1991 things changed and we all moved from our stables and home behind the used-car lot to a very different setting, our present yard on the Cholmondeley Estate. The surroundings were a far cry from those at Upper Aughton Rd, alongside the railway level-crossing, but there undoubtedly was a degree of melancholy attached to our departure from the place at which so many of our dreams had amazingly become reality. But we had all grown older, and the children were now adults. *Red Rum* was at last put out to grass among the rich pastures of the lovely Cheshire countryside.

Throughout his career, 'Rummy' had become a much-travelled gentleman. Quite apart from his 110 races, his time journeying to these fixtures and to countless functions would have surely been enough to exhaust the hardiest of souls. Yet, true to form he just thrived on it. Had it not been for prior commit-ments, he would have been an international rover, for he had been invited to both the USA and Australia.

Even if our new home lacked the glamour of those far-off countries, three former Grand National winners had been prepared within just a few miles of Cholmondeley. The 1949 victor, *Russian Hero*, had been sent out from George

(left) **Morning constitutional** Returning from an early-morning stroll with Joanne McCain in the beautiful Cheshire countryside, *Red Rum* attracts the attention of his admiring neighbours.

(next page)
The perfect combination 'Ginger' and 'Rummy' in relaxed and reflective mood far away from the roar of the crowd.

Owen's Malpas yard, where such great jockeys as Tim Brookshaw, Stan Mellor and Dick Francis had learned their craft. At Whitchurch, the shock 100/1 winner of 1928, *Tipperary Tim*, had been trained, and at Tarporley, *Gamecock*, the hero of the 1887 race received his schooling. This was, therefore, in my mind at least, the ideal place to bring an old warhorse such as *Red Rum*, to a land steeped in the traditions of an event whose history he had totally re-written.

News reader and news maker
BBC television personality Angela Rippon partners *Red Rum* on a morning stroll on Southport Beach in 1980.

(far left)
Tribute to a champion
The Philip Blacker statue of the triple Grand National winner *Red Rum*, near the paddock at Aintree.

(left) **Cast in bronze**
Former jockey Philip Blacker nears completion of his statue of the record-breaking Grand National winner. In his former profession, Philip came third in the great race on *Royal Mail* in 1981 and fourth with *Royal Stuart* 12 months earlier.

Centre stage
Red Rum surrounded by his fans on the occasion of the unveiling of his statue at Aintree in 1988.

CHAPTER FIVE

Is it the end?

The birthday boy

Honoured by the Aintree
Racecourse Company, which
put on a special race meeting
in order to celebrate his 30th
birthday, *Red Rum* joins in the
party atmosphere.

With the frailty that inevitably accompanies advancing age, we drastically cut back on the requests for *Red Rum* to appear at public functions, thus allowing the old boy more time to relax and enjoy the serenity of his new surroundings. By this time, he had been on a daily dosage of eight grams of Warfarin for some years, which made us all very aware that we could lose him at any time. Sadly, that eventuality came very close at the beginning of 1992.

The poor old fellow was extremely ill, at a very low ebb, lying prone in his box and we all feared the worst – that his time had come. It was a dreadful time for everyone at the yard, with tears never far from the surface and none of us able or willing to visualize a single day without *Red Rum* there, so crucial a part of all of us had he become. Purely through his own incredible, indomitable spirit, *Red Rum* survived, answering the silent prayers of so many.

By way of some form of convalescence, Beryl and Joanne travelled with him to County Kilkenny, Ireland, back to the place of his birth, the stud of Martin J McEnery, the very man who had bred him all those years before. Perhaps it was the magic of the emerald isle, or the new and old friends he met while he was there, but he returned in much greater heart than we'd seen him for some time. So much so that he was fit enough once more to lead the parade at Aintree for the Grand National, in which his stable-companion, *Hotplate*, ran a great race until calling it a day at the second last fence.

Back home, *Red Rum* enjoyed being regularly led by Joanne down the quiet lanes, the tranquillity worlds apart from those days of glory when the spruce flew about him, the rolling jockeys scampered to safety and he resisted all adversaries to be first at the winning post. One can but imagine what thoughts ran through the mind of that brave old horse, on those walks with a young woman whose family he had become a part of those long years ago. Years through which he shared their hardships and provided their joy.

His weakness for polo mints was a well-known fact and together with the countless get-well cards, letters of goodwill and Christmas cards sent to him, came always a bountiful supply of the 'mint with the hole' from so many kind fans, near and far. Even at his new home, which is a little bit off the beaten track, people would arrive to see him, stroke him and always they would have with them his favourite delicacy, that green and white wrapped tube.

He fulfilled his Aintree duties in 1993, before the Grand National that was declared void, and again in 1994, when that very fine jockey Richard Dunwoody rode his second Grand National winner aboard Liverpudlian Freddie Starr's *Miinnehoma*. He did, however, appear a little unlike his usual self that day, and by now we knew that he was also being plagued by bouts of arthritis. So it was with great regret that the decision was taken not to submit the old chap to any more discomfort. For the first time since his enforced retirement, the parade of runners for the 1995 Grand National went past the stands without *Red Rum* leading them on.

Later in that month of April we did relent, since he seemed all right in himself, and allowed him to attend a charity organized to raise funds for a young lady jockey badly injured in a fall at Hereford. As always at such functions, he was a tremendous success and came home looking quite fit for a horse of his age.

We were all delighted when we were told by the executive of Aintree racecourse that, to mark the 30th birthday of *Red Rum* on 3 May 1995, they were putting on an evening race-meeting in his honour, and that five of the races that

Now that looks nice

Watching his birthday cake being cut, there is no doubt in *Red Rum*'s mind just who it's intended for.

night were named after him. The other event was to bear the name of the lucky devil privileged to have been associated with *Red Rum* for so many years of utter magic – yours truly.

It really was a splendid occasion, the racecourse did us all proud that night, when for once, in a carnival-like party atmosphere, racing took second place. The majority of the 7000-odd crowd were attending a race-meeting for the first time in their lives and were there plainly and simply to see the living legend, *Red*

The saddest farewell

In the shadow of the Grand National winning post, Mrs Beryl McCain spends some memory-filled moments at her beloved *Red Rum*'s grave. 20 October 1995.

Rum. A giant-sized birthday cake was on display, complete with 30 candles, and the people were overjoyed when '*Rummy*' tentatively approached it, stretched out his nose for an inspection and, when satisfied, began nibbling away at it. He thrilled them all, walking around and around the paddock for them to gaze devotedly at him, posing over and over for his fans to take photographs and allowing even the smallest and noisiest children to nuzzle up to him and stroke his once well-muscled form. It was the perfect setting and occasion for what we were not to know was *Red Rum*'s very last public appearance.

On the morning of Wednesday 18 October 1995, my son Donald found *Red Rum* flat out in his box, unable to rise and very obviously in a distressed condition. He immediately informed me and straight off I knew it was the end, that awful moment we'd all been dreading. I called our vet John Burgess right away and, like the fine man he is, he was with us within minutes. We both entered *Red Rum*'s box and by this time the old boy was standing, with Jo and Donald anxiously beside him. But he was very wobbly and it was pitiful to see him looking so terribly ill. We were all crying unashamedly, despite individual attempts to contain ourselves.

John examined him with a tenderness that was revealing and for which we will all remain grateful, and then expressed the opinion that the old fellow had probably had a heart attack during the night. His circulation was failing rapidly and he wasn't going to last much longer. There was only one course of action open to us and, thinking about it, I suppose you could say that *Red Rum* made the decision for us.

Each of the yard staff spent a few seconds in the box, saying their own personal goodbyes to the one horse they adored above all others, until there remained just Joanne, John Burgess and myself left kneeling with 'that one good horse'. His head cradled in the girl's arms, with those ever-curious eyes wide in understanding was one of the saddest sights one could ever witness. Then Jo fled from the stable in tears, no longer able to withhold her grieving.

Final resting place

A melancholy moment for both Beryl McCain and Joe McNally, Aintree Racecourse Marketing Manager, at *Red Rum*'s graveside.

It was then my turn. I slipped one last polo mint into his mouth and, at that one time when I had resolved to remain with this wonderful friend of so many hard-fought years, to my everlasting regret I chickened out. I asked John if he minded if I left, and with a sympathetic glance he just said:

'No, it's all right Ginger, you just pop off outside now.'

I did and at 8 o'clock that morning a solitary shot rang out marking the passing of an era, a legend and the truest friend anyone could hope for.

For 23 years, *Red Rum* had been an indefinable part of my life and the lives of those closest to me and the numbness I now felt was just overpowering. Then I ventured back into his box for one final sight of '*Rummy*' and was amazed to see him, just as I had so many times in the past, with that proud neck arched and taut and with his ears cocked in that strange inquisitive way he had.

Hallowed ground

The grave of *Red Rum,* along-side the winning post at Aintree racecourse.

We informed Aintree of the sad news and the staff there were brilliant, at once preparing for his arrival as we had agreed some years before. The horse box arrived, the lads gently and with such touching reverence placed him inside and then the ramp was closed and he was driven slowly away. He was going for the final time to Aintree, the home of the Grand National, and I suppose one could also say the spiritual home of *Red Rum*. It was a journey he knew so well, but this time it was one from which he was not to return.

Some hours later, a message was relayed to me from Bob Dixon, the race-course foreman. 'Tell Ginger we've laid *Red Rum* to rest with dignity, in the shadow of the winning post. And he's facing the right way.' That was very nice, and typical of that tough breed of Geordie men. We were also informed that the Union flag above the Queen Mother Stand had been lowered to half mast.

The tributes just poured in, bringing tender sentiments and such comforting words at a time when the consideration of so many meant a very great deal to us. Among the many it is difficult to choose, so these are but a random sample.

From Jackie Grainger: '*Red Rum* was a Christian of a horse – the best I ever looked after. I rode him out regularly and he used to be a real wind-up because he would kick and buck on the road leading to the beach. But there was never any fear of being unseated because it was like sitting in an armchair. There will never be another *Red Rum*.'

From Jenny Pitman: 'He was a great servant to racing, one of life's characters. He'd been there and done it. It is a sad day for all of us.'

From Peter O'Sullevan: 'It was one of the privileges of one's life to have called *Red Rum* home to all his Aintree victories, especially the hat-trick.'

From Peter Scudamore: 'The only time I ever rode *Red Rum* was at a chari-ty function. Even though I have sat on thousands of horses, it was still an hon-our to pay homage to the one who has won the Grand National more times than any other.'

There were so many more, equally kind and full of praise for the horse whose life had touched so many in the most wondrous of ways. Then came the letters from the general public, thousands of ordinary people from all walks of life tak-ing the time to convey their sadness, their concern for us and their undying affection for an animal who had come to mean so much to them. His grave at Aintree was laid out with such care, covered with a deep carpet of flowers and wreaths and encompassed within a small white fence. Many thousands of people travelled great distances in the days after his burial to attend the grave and place their own floral tributes to him.

For us back across the Mersey, it remained a time of great loss and enormous sadness and it will, I suppose for some time yet, but we have so many wonderful memories to remind us of how extremely fortunate we were to have *Red Rum* as a part of our lives for so long.

I was also particularly fortunate in having such people beside me along the way, people who made the tasks we faced much easier. Billy Ellison, Jackie Grainger, Billy Beardwood and the finest farrier in the land, Bob Marshall, whose skilful care, together with the Southport sea, saved 'Rummy' from the crippling foot disease. Brian Fletcher, Tommy Stack and Ron Barry, his jockeys who so many times shared with *Red Rum* the dangers of the Chase. And of course, the one person without whom none of our endeavours would have been possible, dear Beryl, to whom I owe so much.

Red Rum's record stands forever supreme in the annals of racing, and although his time record was bettered in the 1990 Grand National, the course by that time had been drastically modified, rendering it considerably less severe than before. To go out for five successive years in the toughest horse race on earth, and perform as he did, was truly a testament to his great heart and enormous fighting spirit. But to win the Grand National three times, I think, requires an explanation from the gods. However, I feel that his amazing appeal to the people is a little less difficult to understand. Ordinary men and women were somehow able to identify with *Red Rum*, to relate to his humble origins, understand the harsh rigours he endured in his life, and to rejoice and take hope from his brilliance. He inspired them in a way few others creatures were able to do, and in a very dramatic and positive way.

Red Rum arrived at precisely the right time, for me, for himself and, most of all perhaps, for the Grand National itself. At the very moment the Grand National appeared through apathy and neglect to be lost, with its future in constant doubt, he blazed a glorious trail across that racecourse and, thankfully, aroused the belief that the race and those who compete in it were worthy of better things. Through three eras of Aintree history – the Tophams, Bill Davies and Ladbrokes – *Red Rum* secured the future of the race for us all in a manner never to be forgotten.

Yet still, through all these achievements he did more than win the Grand National three times. He won a place in the hearts of people everywhere. This is certainly the greatest prize, for it is one that is beyond value.

Thanks for the memories *Red Rum*.

They will live forever.

(following pages)

The spirit of Aintree

The setting sun silhouettes the permanent reminder to all of the very best in sporting endeavour. Many thanks *Red Rum*.

First published in Great Britain in 1996 by

George Weidenfeld & Nicolson Ltd

The Orion Publishing Group

Orion House

5 Upper St Martin's Lane

London

WC2H 9EA

A catalogue record for this book is available from the British Library.

ISBN 0 297 83609 9

Designed by Leigh Jones

Printed and bound by Butler and Tanner Ltd, Frome and London

Picture Credits

All photographs are © *Donald McCain* except as stated below:

14, 62, 92 © *Allsport*

15, 23, 29, 42, 48 (bottom), 49, 54, 58, 85 (top) © *Gerry Cranham*

19, 20, 32, 34, 35, 37, 38, 43, 44, 61, 63, 71, 79, 82 © *Harry Ormersher*

39, 51, 53, 60, 83, 84 © *Colorsport*

48 (top), 50, 55, 68, 69-70, 75 © *George Selwyn*

64 © *Popperfoto*

Front jacket photograph, 85 (bottom) © *Rex Features*

88, 89, 90, 91, 93, 94-5 © *Thomas Howard*